GOD'S PROMISES THAT
KEEP US

God's Promises That Keep Us

J. Ellsworth Kalas

Abingdon Press
Nashville

GOD'S PROMISES THAT KEEP US

Copyright © 2010 by Abingdon Press

This book is printed on acid-free paper.

Library of Congress Cataloging-in-Publication Data

Kalas, J. Ellsworth, 1923-
God's promises that keep us / J. Ellsworth Kalas.
    p.   cm.
ISBN 978-1-4267-1003-2 (trade paperback : alk. paper)
1. Promises—Religious aspects—Christianity. 2. God (Christianity)—Promises. 3. Bible—Theology. I. Title.
BS680.P68K36 2010
248.8'6—dc22

2010030305

10 11 12 13 14 15 16 17 18 19—10 9 8 7 6 5 4 3 2 1

MANUFACTURED IN THE UNITED STATES OF AMERICA

CONTENTS

GOD'S PROMISES THAT KEEP US

Sometimes those of us who write books can tell when a certain book was first conceived, while sometimes when someone asks we can only wave an apologetic hand as we answer, "It's hard to say."

In the case of this book, I can tell you not only *when* it came to birth but also *where*. It was in a quite modest kitchen at 1506 Center Street in Sioux City, Iowa, over a period of years in the late 1930s. On a shelf in that kitchen, just above the stove, was a box of cards, each measuring roughly one by three inches, each one containing a verse from the Bible. The box was popularly referred to as "precious promises." I don't know if that was the name the publisher gave to the collection or if it was the title earnest Christians had given to such verses long before an enterprising publisher organized a specific collection into printed form; I only know how sacred and beloved the box was to my mother and to untold thousands of other persons at that time.

It isn't quite fair to refer to the box as a "promise box," because the verses really constituted a way of approaching life, an earnest attempt to bring oneself into union with God. The verses covered a wide area of biblical teaching. Many had a quality of admonition and instruction, but the overall mood was one of encouragement. Those who kept such a box in easy reach were sustained by the contents. Some verses took on such personal significance that they were laid aside, on top of the box or beside it, to be looked at more often. Mind you, the owner of the box knew such verses by heart, but there was a peculiar strength in looking at the printed form and holding it in one's hand.

I suspect that secular students of religious practices might write off the use of those cards as superstition. Quite certainly they might hold in criticism, perhaps even in amusement, my mother's habit of taking a card from the box each day as her "promise for the day." I might entertain such a criticism if this were my mother's only tie to the Bible. But by the time she took her "promise for the day," she already would have prayed on her knees and read a longer portion from the Bible.

I had no idea in those long-ago years that I would someday write a book about that box and specifically about some of those promises. I revered the promises because they meant so much to my parents, especially my mother, and because on several occasions I had seen how uniquely appropriate a particular verse proved to be at a particular time.

That particular Center Street box has now been lost for half a century or more, so I can't promise that the verses I embrace in this book were all in that box. The verses in this book are verses that have blessed me over the years. I dare to hope and believe that some or all of them will give a lift or an insight to you. Some have become significant to me in times of pain, some in joy. Some seem especially appropriate to the era of the Great Depression, when they were so "precious" in our household. It's just possible, therefore, that they will mean something very special to someone in a current crisis. Some of these Bible verses took on new meaning during World War II. In this world where wars seem to reappear with sad frequency, those words speak to us still.

When you read this book, I'm very sure you will think of a verse that is priceless to you, and you'll wonder why it's not in this book. You may even write or e-mail me to ask me why. The verse may mean so much to you that perhaps you will reprimand me, even if kindly, for not including it. If you do, I'll understand. I'll just know that, whether or not you've ever seen a box of "precious promises," you have discovered that there are promises that keep us. And I will thank God with you that you have found it to be so.

—J. Ellsworth Kalas

CHAPTER 1

NO FEAR OF THE DARK

The LORD *is my light and my salvation; / whom shall I fear?*
(Psalm 27:1)

If you visit me in my seminary office, you will find a wall hanging with this centuries-old English prayer:

> From
> Ghoulies and Ghosties and
> Long Leggity Beasties
> and other things that go
> Bump in the night
> Good Lord—Deliver us.

I like that! The quaint language makes me smile, even as I try to capture more fully the pictures it evokes. I don't give much thought to ghoulies and ghosties and long-leggity beasties, but I think I understand those who did—and those who do. The ancient soul who wrote that prayer was afraid of the dark and of whatever creatures might inhabit the dark. And so it is with us all, at one time or another in our lives, especially when we extend the meaning of the "dark" to those aspects of our future that are unknown—and by that very token, threatening. We may describe our fears in different, and by our judgment more sophisticated, language than that used by the unknown medieval soul. One

1

of the gifts of modern psychology is that it gives us pseudonyms for what our ancestors described in mystical or superstitious terms. But the fear is there—the fear of the dark. And all of us sometimes have to walk in the dark. Every one of us.

So it is that I love the testimony of an ancient saint. I want to claim the promise of that testimony for my life and for yours, just as others have for several thousand years:

> The LORD is my light and my salvation;
> whom shall I fear? (Psalm 27:1)

If your Bible carries notations over the psalms, it classifies this psalm as one of the many attributed specifically to King David, the sweet singer of Israel. If that tradition be true— a conclusion I am happy to accept—it is easy to imagine a long list of instances when David might have spoken these words. Indeed, I suspect that he spoke them not once but many times over the long and varied years of his life, perhaps beginning as a shepherd boy protecting his flock against a wild beast and continuing to a day in old age when he looked back on some of the errors of his life with the kind of shudder that only the past can evoke.

Some of the psalms tell us the circumstances under which the psalm was written. This one leaves that question to our imagination. The psalm offers us enough details, however, that we can imagine David in a variety of dark and threatening places. One thinks naturally of David the military man, a warrior in the storied traditions of the past, since in the psalm he speaks of enemies and foes that have threatened "to devour my flesh" (27:2). Was he recalling the day he challenged the giant Goliath, who boasted, "Come to me, and I will give your flesh to the birds of the air and to the wild animals of the field" (1 Samuel 17:44)? Or might the words in Psalm 27:1 refer to those occasions when David was fleeing from the armies of King Saul, compelled repeatedly to hide in wilderness caves? Or perhaps that even darker night (conceivably the worst of all) many years later when David was pursued by the armies led by his own son Absalom, who had mounted a revolt against him? The words of this psalm—"Though an army encamp against me, / my heart shall not fear" (27:3)—would fit any of those occasions.

Whatever the specifics, this psalm comes from someone who was familiar with peril. One can almost hear the sword and shield crashing beneath the rhythm of the psalmist's words. And remember this too: whatever the circumstances when first these words were recorded, this is a song to be sung on life's battlefield. It is not the product of a scholar's research in the library or a dilettante's parlor, nor did it come from a philosophical discussion group. A host has encamped around this soul or is likely to do so at any moment; war has been declared on the writer and he sees no avenue of escape, before or behind, left or right. Yet in such an hour he knows this: "The Lord is my light and my salvation; / whom shall I fear?"

But as all of us know, there are battlefields of life beyond those of armed conflict—and indeed, there are weapons of destruction beyond those issued by military headquarters. We have become increasingly conscious of this fact as we converse with persons who have returned from Iraq or Afghanistan or other areas of conflict, or as we read studies of their experiences. Thousands of modern Davids have discovered that they must cope with worse enemies after they return from the battlefield than ever they met in armed conflict. On the battlefield they had defense weapons of their own, and the enemy was human and perhaps visible. But these enemies that come now in the middle of the night or in the sound of an errant automobile or a playful firecracker—for these a defense is hard to find because the enemy is so difficult to conceive and confront: the enemy called fear.

And there are human enemies off the military battlefield. David spoke of such: "False witnesses have risen against me" (27:12). Life has few battles worse than when people tell lies about us—or indeed, tell unwelcome truth in the hope of discrediting us, for sometimes the truth, too, can destroy unless it is dealt with mercy. And when the witnesses, as in the psalmist's story, are false, there seems no means of defense; we enter the battle with hands tied at our backs.

As we read between the lines on this psalm, we sense that David may have been wrestling with still another kind of darkness. When he pleads, "Do not turn your servant away in anger, / you who have been my help. / Do not cast me off, do not forsake me, / O God of my salvation" (27:9), we realize that David is faced by a common spiritual problem: just when he needs God the most, he thinks that perhaps God has turned against him. This is a quite natural reaction to hard times. We are susceptible to the suggestion that God must be unhappy with us, else why would we be in such a bad state? We think that the darkness is a result of our sins or our bad judgment.

And in truth, it is highly possible that the mess we're in is, indeed, our own fault. It may be that we're in the dark because, so to speak, we've turned out the lights. But even if our troubles are of our own doing, and even if we have complicated our problems by our attitude toward the God who would help us, this is no reason to think that God has forsaken us or is inclined unfavorably toward us. Fortunately, there is grace with God. Light and salvation: these are the very nature of God. We need therefore to set our eyes on God's nature rather than on our own errant ways. Mind you, we need to face up to ourselves and to repent. But we need then to move on into a healthy recognition that God is on our side and is more prepared to help us than we are to receive help.

Roughly a generation ago Edinburgh University's distinguished psychologist G. M. Carstairs addressed a meeting of the National Association of Mental Health in London. He declared that fear was the great threat to mental health in his generation.[1] I'm quite sure the psychologist's diagnosis would not have changed for this twenty-first century. I don't like to speculate on comparative conditions from one generation to the next, but I suspect that the power of fear is, if anything, even more present now than a generation ago. Perhaps this is because we continue to read of remedies and hopeful prospects only to discover that these remedies have been oversold or that if they have succeeded, somehow our maladies have become more complicated so that the miracle remedies no longer work. We are free from the Black Plague of the Middle Ages, but each autumn we wonder what new strain of flu will appear, quite out of nowhere it seems, and with the specter of being beyond current cures. Not many of us worry about ghoulies and ghosties, but we discover that we have fears of our own and that they are just as frightening as anything our ancestors knew.

And for some the night is so long. That brilliant but tortured soul, the novelist F. Scott Fitzgerald, wrote, "In a real dark night of the soul it is always three o'clock in the morning."[2] If the dark could be restricted to certain hours, if one could be assured that when daybreak comes the darkness will disappear, the darkness could be endured. But if it is as Fitzgerald experienced it, so that it is always three o'clock in the morning, what then? What if even when you're walking in the glory of midday sun the darkness is still impenetrable: what then?

It is then that we need God's promise, the promise spelled out for us by the ancient poet. "The LORD is my *light!*" You and I need a light that has nothing to do with the hour on the clock and indeed nothing to do with the power supplies of our best human contraptions. Because, as you know, the elements of darkness that are most powerful are quite beyond any electrical system. A flashlight would have lit up David's cave better than his flickering lamp, but the flashlight would also have raised larger areas of shadow. Our knowledge expands our defenses and at the same moment magnifies our perils.

So we need God's light. Sometimes the light reveals that there was no actuality in the darkness. The squeak in the floor that we thought was doom creeping toward us proves in the light to have been nothing more than the normal settling in of floor joists. That physical symptom that we thought would have a "three months to live" diagnosis proves in the light of the doctor's examination to be "a routine thing. No problem at all." So often the light reveals that the darkness wasn't real—or at least that it wasn't permanent.

But what if the light falls on some dark corner where we find there really *is* a long-leggity beastie? Suppose the light reveals that the problem is not imaginary but very real and very big. Suppose the doctor's examination carries with it a quiet shaking of the head, or the response to your employment application is a form letter of rejection. Then what? I think of a cartoon: a man in an optometrist's office is appealing to the examiner, "I'd like to see things a little less clearly, please." Some of us have known times like that. What if the clear light—the light of the Lord, indeed!—reveals things we'd rather not see?

The promise of the scripture is as good as ever. It is not the circumstance that matters but the *light and the salvation.* It strikes me that the psalmist never really said that God took away the threat. Rather, God blessed this ancient believer with faith that conquered the fear. The light of God puts our problems in perspective. The divine light takes our problems out of the realm of human speculation—which tends so easily to be negative even to the point of foolishness—and brings them into the diminishing setting of reality. They are problems, yes, but they are not disasters. They are issues to be met, not forces to which we must surrender.

I would not be worthy of your time if I denied the reality of some of our long-leggity beasties. Life has its trials and its sorrows, its low places and its heartbreaks, its betrayals and its shattering disappointments. None of us can ever escape them all. But we need not fear them—not if the Lord is our light and our salvation. In his light we will be delivered from the fear of the dark, from the unreasoning and irrational fear that paralyzes our power to stand up and fight. And by God's salvation we are led through conquest into triumph. God not only sheds light on our path so that we can see things for what they are and can recognize that the ghosties are only shadows of a harmless twig, God also empowers us to deal with the realities and to win. When the enemy is real, God's light puts the enemy in perspective so we can see that our divine resources are greater than any trouble we encounter.

And how does God deliver our salvation? The possibilities range from the sublime to the absurd. Most often the salvation comes through people—sometimes people who we knew were on our side but just as often, I think, through people who are surprise aides. I remember a member of my parish who lost a deeply cherished wife, the kind of person who provided more daily sustenance than her husband knew until she was gone and the sustenance with her. We counseled on several occasions, and I prayed for him often, both in his presence and in my personal prayer times.

He told me a year or two later that the prayers hadn't really helped. Nothing helped until a new friend came into his life, he said—not a person he would marry, but one who provided companionship and a daily telephone call. This was what helped him, he said, when prayer had failed to do so.

I marvel still at my dullness of spirit that I failed to explain to my friend that more often than not the person who makes the difference is the answer to our prayers. God works almost always—preferably, I think—through human agents. What the man needed was not a thunderbolt from heaven, not necessarily a mystical experience: he needed a substitute for what he had lost, a human presence. I failed to explain the obvious to my friend, that God so often delivers salvation through human beings.

And as I said a moment ago, the means of salvation can be from sublime to absurd. The Old Testament book of Numbers tells of a day when a donkey gave counsel to a high-priced consultant (Numbers 22:22-35). Many homes for persons under long-term care report that a visit from a trained, wonderfully compassionate dog carries emotional healing. Some in a dark night recall a song, long-forgotten, that becomes angel music for that moment. Others recall a phrase a mother or a grandfather used to speak. And often—perhaps every time the sacred Meal is celebrated—people find divine intervention as they receive Holy Communion. Believe me, the carriers of salvation are as varied as the circumstances that demand them.

I love the vigor with which that long-ago poet declared his faith. There's a grand kind of divine audacity in the way most translations give us this verse: "The LORD is my light and my salvation; / whom shall I fear?" I like that rhetorical question. I see the believer standing on his or her little plot of faith and throwing a challenge into the teeth of the universe. It's as if the writer is saying to some unknown opponent, "List those things that I should fear. Give me your worst catalog of terror if you will. Which one do you think will frighten me?"

And I remember then stories from people I have known, real people in real trouble. There was this alcoholic who for so long dreaded every social engagement where he would have to struggle to say no to the offer of a drink—until one day he got the infusion of divine self-confidence that made him smile at his own former insecurity. I think of a woman who always lost heart when circumstances took a particular turn. Then she grasped that the Lord was her light and salvation, so that when those circumstances went bump in the night she could accept the bumping as a drum beat of triumph.

Obviously I can't know what is in your mind in those hours—the three-o'clock-in-the-morning hours that can come at any time of the day or night—when the long-leggity beasties pursue you. But this I do know, by personal experience and by the thousands of witnesses who have come my way: there is light and there is salvation, for you and for me, in God. You can say with the poet of so long ago, "I will fear no one." It's a promise that will keep you.

NOTES

1. Leonard Griffith, *God in Man's Experience* (Waco, Tex.: Word Books, 1968), 39.
2. Justin Kaplan, ed., *Barlett's Familiar Quotations,* 16th ed. (Boston: Little, Brown, and Co., 1992), 694.

CHAPTER 2

MY EXPERIENCE WITH TROUBLE

When I was in trouble, I called to the Lord, / and he answered me. (Psalm 120:1 GNT)

In my years of living and learning, I have become fascinated with the variety of authorities that hold forth in our world. The range is marvelous to behold. Most authorities are known only within their field of expertise. When I was a graduate student at Harvard University, I walked in common company with authorities, because in a great university authorities are a stock in trade, like diamond necklaces in a jewelry store. One of the highly regarded at Harvard was a professor who was considered the world authority on Philo of Alexandria, a first-century scholar. I confess that Philo hadn't played a major role in my intellectual life prior to that time, but I always looked with awe on that professor after I learned that he was the stated authority on Philo. At a decidedly different level, I recall a day in my boyhood when my father pointed to a man and said, "That's Peterson. There's nobody in Sioux City that knows more about running the washroom of a laundry than he does." I watched the man moving from one steaming tub to another and figured that I was in the presence of greatness. Experts come in a variety of shapes and sizes, and I won't minimize an authority in a field in which I have no expertise. There was a time when I had an area of authority. For some time in my years as a parish pastor, I came to feel that I was an authority on *trouble*. It isn't that I had experienced an extraordinary variety of trouble firsthand, but I was a good pastoral listener and I learned a very great deal about trouble by being willing to listen to the burdens carried by others. I wasn't really a trouble-shooter; I was more of a trouble-sitter. People came to me with troubles that were often beyond cure, so they weren't hoping for deliverance but for a compassionate ear and heart.

The book of Psalms is probably the most-loved book in the Bible. This is true for many reasons, but I suspect that the major appeal for vast numbers of people is that the writers of the Psalms were people who knew something about trouble. Sometimes they were deep in trouble even as they wrote, so deep that you can almost feel the muck of their quicksand pulling you down. In other instances they write in triumph, grateful to God for having been delivered from trouble. "Misery loves company" is surely one of the most popular proverbs in the English language. The *Oxford Dictionary of Quotations* identifies it as coming from the sixteenth century, but of course that only refers to the first record of its being in print. I suspect the human race was very young when someone first discovered this truth about trouble, that one feels better for finding a fellow sufferer. Well, the book of Psalms has many such fellow sufferers, and one who had found a remedy told his story in a succinct sentence: "When I was in trouble, I called to the LORD, / and he answered me" (Psalm 120:1). That's the way the Good News Translation puts it. The King James Version finds a stronger word for trouble: "In my distress I cried unto the LORD, and he heard me."

We don't know who wrote those words. Perhaps that's all the better. We recognize this person simply as our near kin in human experience. One of the characters in Thornton Wilder's classic play *Our Town* comments on the human story from her place in the village cemetery, "I never realized before how troubled and how—how in the dark live persons are.... From morning till night, that's all they are—troubled."[1] I've talked with some of the folks Wilder refers to. For them, trouble needs to be spelled with a capital T, because for them Trouble has become personified, as if it were a living, breathing thing, more real than God or the morning sunlight. Trouble can do that to a person.

What kind of trouble? That depends on the person. I have a feeling that our susceptibility to different kinds of trouble is as varied as our susceptibility to different types of physical ills. Our life experiences and our family heritages make us open to particular kinds of trouble—for some people, financial; for others, marital; for still others, vocational. And that's only a beginning of the list. When you visit a new physician you're generally asked to fill out a form regarding your medical history. In the instances of some illnesses the form asks whether your mother or your father had such an illness, or if some sibling was so afflicted, suggesting that some diseases may run in the family. I'm quite sure this is true of certain breeds of trouble: you see their recurrance in a given family from generation to generation.

The person who wrote Psalm 120 seemed especially to have *people* trouble. That's one of the worst kinds of trouble because it's so hard to escape it. People are everywhere, and while there may be times in many of our lives when we'd like to retreat to a desert island for a while, most of us want to see people at least once in a while, and some of us want to see them a great deal. If people become a source of trouble, the structures of daily life hang in the balance.

So listen to this ancient soul in trouble:

> Woe is me, that I am an alien in Meshech,
>   that I must live among the tents of Kedar.
> Too long have I had my dwelling

among those who hate peace.
I am for peace;
but when I speak,
they are for war. (120:5-7)

The references to Meshech and Kedar are interesting. The two areas were very far apart, so far that it's almost certain the writer never actually lived in both. The people of Meshech, residing between the Black and Caspian Seas, were known as a barbarous people, while the Kedar were a nomadic, unfriendly people who roamed the desert of the Arabian Peninsula. Think, if you can, of two groups of people who are currently known for a kind of endemic unfriendliness, a disposition set always on hostility, and you'll understand what the psalmist was saying. He felt he had lived all his life with people who wanted conflict. "I am for peace,/ but when I speak, / they are for war."

I wonder if perhaps the psalmist was speaking figuratively. Might he have been talking about people in his own neighborhood, perhaps his own synagogue, who seemed to him to be so difficult that he chose to describe them as the kind of ethnic group known for their unpleasant ways? Or was he engaged in a time of self-pity? Was he saying, "I try to get along with folks, but they just don't give me a chance."

Well, the issue is not whether the fault is in the people with whom we associate or whether it is lodged within our own temperament; it's still trouble, whether someone causes it for me or whether I make the trouble for myself. Some observers of the human scene feel that trouble with people is the worst trouble of all. We can endure sickness, financial distress, even failure if only there are friends who will stand by, people who will understand and empathize. But when people are cold, indifferent, or antagonistic, life can be nearly impossible to manage. And it isn't just our friends or family members who can touch the hot switch in our lives. Sometimes a clerk in a store can do it or the driver in a passing automobile. People trouble is very big trouble, and probably all of us are susceptible to it.

But someone who is going through a lost job or a pressing mortgage will tell you that financial troubles are even worse. The late James Cash Penney saw his department store empire brought to the brink of disaster and his own millions wiped out. In the process, however, Mr. Penney came to a new relationship with God and eventually to a rebuilding of his life in general and of his financial structures in particular. But for a while he thought his life had ended or was about to end in the sanitorium where he was sent for recovery.

When I think of financial trouble I think of an evening some seventy years ago when my father and I walked to a coal company a block or two down Center Street to buy two bushels of coal, pulling it up the street in a coaster wagon. It would be fuel enough, Dad said, to keep us warm through the night and part of the next day, when he hoped there'd be money enough to buy half a ton of coal. That's financial trouble, and its impress is still on my soul.

But someone else will remind us that financial troubles are nothing to be compared with health problems. "If you're healthy, you can handle almost anything," they say—and most of us wouldn't argue the question. Almost everyone has passing encounters with illness, but some get more than their share. As a pastor I've known some folks who when I visited them in the hospital greeted me by saying, with gallows humor, "I'll bet you're tired of seeing me here, aren't you?" Some families seem dedicated to keeping the medical profession in business. "The hospital should put your name over their new wing," I once told a person, "because your family has almost paid for it." One can joke when the illness ends in recovery, but in some cases there's very little to joke about, even for the most upbeat souls. It's just heartbreak. Trouble, trouble, trouble.

I'm a bit of a sentimentalist, so I'll add to trouble's list *romantic* trouble. This can begin when you're still in grade school and fall in love with your teacher. I suspect there's something philosophically significant about that in its utterly irrational quality. So often our problems of the heart spring from matters far out of our control or out of the realm of reason. Most of us have, at some point or another in life, loved someone without being loved in return—or have been loved by someone whom we couldn't love, so we felt guilty for not being able to return the feeling in measure. And some remember being ready to marry, then suddenly feeling unsure about their feelings or sensing an unexpected attraction to another person. Then there's the matter of loving someone so fully only to lose them by death or divorce or betrayal. Friend, this is trouble. It breaks your heart in such private places that you can't easily share the pain with anyone else. And trouble is always worse when you can't share it with at least one person.

So what kind of trouble do you have? "All kinds," the sad-faced man answers, "and I brought most of it on myself." I understand. I'm a specialist in that kind of trouble. As I ponder the course of my life I conclude that the devil probably hasn't worried about sending trouble to me because I have managed to produce a good supply for myself. A lion's share of my troubles have been homemade. Perhaps you're in the same category. If so, you'll find some consolation in what the psalmist has written. He doesn't make a distinction between troubles that are our own doing and those that have been caused by others. Neither does the psalmist suggest that God will make a distinction so that some of our troubles will be relieved since they're not our fault while others will have to be suffered through since we brought them on ourselves. I'm grateful God doesn't have such a system of classifying troubles and the degree to which divine help will be extended.

So what do we do with trouble? We don't become experts in trouble by the amount of trouble we suffer or by observing it in others any more than one becomes a physician by being sick for a lifetime. Some people have an inordinate amount of trouble yet are always amateurs in handling it. The expert in trouble is the person who has learned how to handle trouble—especially how to put it to some good end. And what was the formula for this long-ago expert in trouble? "In my trouble," he said, "I cried..." (NASB). I have interrupted his statement in order to comment that this portion of the person's approach was natural and normal. Not particularly noble or imaginative, but normal. But at least it's a starting place and not to be brushed aside. I say this because I've known some people (in truth, I'm one of them) who believe in keeping their troubles to themselves. By doing so, they shut out the possibility that another person might have some answers—and that, at the very least, our pain might be relieved in some measure simply by speaking it aloud to another individual.

But as I said, I interrupted the report. The wise soul continues, "I cried *to the* LORD" (NASB, emphasis added). It's important to know where to cry, and also to know why you've gone to a particular place of refuge or counsel. The psalmist believed that God had the resources to help and that God had a heart to offer help.

Surveys tell us that the hymn "Amazing Grace" continues year after year to be a favorite with all kinds of people of a wide spread of ages. I've learned that not many of these people can give a reasoned definition of grace, but they sense the essence of it—that God is disposed in their favor, is inclined to hear their cry and to listen sympathetically. They might not spell it out that way, but that's the general idea: God is on their side, willing at the least to listen to them—and not interrupt while they're still trying to formulate exactly what they have in mind.

But another question still asserts itself. If I cry to the Lord when I'm in trouble, what will he do? The ancient poet gave the simplest yet greatest of answers: *and he answered me.*

I like that. When I'm in trouble, I don't care to hear all

17

the whereases, maybes, and in-case-ofs. I want only to know that there's someone in this blessed universe who can hear, who cares, and who is disposed to answer. I don't want to be put on hold while music not of my choosing is played, nor to hear that the supply is exhausted, that I must get my application approved by an assistant investigator, or that my form is filled out incorrectly. When I'm in trouble, I need an answer.

The psalmist never really tells us what the answer was. I expect he considered any such statement superfluous. If you know the nature of God and God's unlimited capacity and power, you don't need to know how or what was the answer. Details, mere details!

Over the years I have thought often of another song composed by someone in trouble. Whether a man or a woman, no one knows. It is part of the great tradition of spirituals that has come to us out of the world of slavery and in some instances of the troubles that followed slavery. Listen:

> Nobody knows the trouble I've seen,
> Nobody knows my sorrow;
> Nobody knows the trouble I've seen,
> Glory! Hallelujah!

What a way to manhandle trouble! End it with a shout. Laugh it to shame. After you've taken full inventory of your troubles and are convinced that no one can really believe your report, tell heaven and hell and the universe, "Glory! Hallelujah!"

There's trouble to be met in this world, no doubt about it. Trouble is no respecter of periods in history or of age, race, creed, success, education, or culture. So what shall we do with it? The psalmist tells us what he did: "When I was in trouble, I called to the LORD, / and he answered me" (GNT). The unknown author of the spiritual looked at her troubles and said, "No one's ever seen so many, so bad:

Glory, hallelujah!" And from my own experience with trouble, both as person and as pastor, I would say, "Amen. Amen. Amen."

NOTE

1. Thornton Wilder, *Our Town,* Act 3 (New York: Coward-McCann, 1938), 74.

CHAPTER 3

A PERFECT DAY, AND WHAT TO DO WITH IT

This is the day that the LORD has made; / let us rejoice and be glad in it. (Psalm 118:24)

Most philosophers have their day and are forgotten, and I'm sure the time will come when only a few will quote Charlie Brown. Still and all, he's had a remarkable run of it, considering that his platform has been the comic page and his picture has made him beloved rather than ridiculed. The world's worst baseball pitcher and everybody's favorite fall guy, he has an uncanny gift for making readers smile as they say, "Poor Charlie Brown"—probably because most of us see ourselves in some of Charlie's troubled days. Once he explained to one of his friends, "I've developed a new philosophy. I only dread one day at a time."

I venture that several million nodded in agreement the day Charlie Brown offered that philosophy. I understood what he was saying. I've known such times. Nevertheless, when I read Charlie's words that day I wanted to introduce him to someone whose name I don't know but whose outlook on life I prize. This is the person (whether man or woman, the Bible doesn't say) who declared, "This is the day that the LORD has made; / let us rejoice and be glad in it."

I won't tell you that this is my favorite verse of the Bible, because it's impossible for me to name a single such verse. But I think I have probably quoted this verse more than any other. For many years I spoke it at the beginning of each day—to myself and to God, with no one around to hear me, which made it all the more sacred because of the privacy with which I was speaking. Sometimes I've said it in unbridled gratitude, feeling I was part of an angel chorus, and sometimes I've said it as a challenge to those demons that were seeking to lay an early claim to the day. But whether in joy or in defiance, this is the spirit in which I wish to live. I no longer quote this verse as a daily ritual, but I cling still to the mood, and I see this verse as one of the loveliest promises in all of scripture.

Before I go further I want to make a disclaimer for the careful Bible student. My commitment to this verse is in its broad, human application. I realize that it was almost surely written originally for a special occasion in the ancient nation of Israel. Some say it was used for King David's enthronement, and others that it was written for the good King Hezekiah. Still others see it as a prophetic statement, related to the crucifixion, the resurrection, and the eventual total victory of our Lord Jesus Christ. There are also those who feel that the verse applies especially to the Sabbath— that is, that the day of ordained rest and worship is the day of which it can especially be said, "This is the day that the LORD has made." I empathize with that interpretation because for years I've been in love with the way John Newton—author of "Amazing Grace"—described Sunday: "Day of all the week the best."

I respect all of the interpretations I have just enumerated, and I am inclined to feel that one or two of them are definitely significant for either the original purpose of the writing or the extended significance as the New Testament reveals it. But it's my intention to talk with you about this verse not at the level of biblical scholarship but at the place of warm religious experience. I see it as the kind of verse that any believer can apply to any and every day. And more than that: I see this verse as one that all of us would be wise to lay claim to every day. That is, make every day a coronation day, a day of unique significance—because under God, every day *is* potentially a day of unique significance. Every day has its own inimitable soul print, and certainly every day is a divine gift.

When we approach a day with such an attitude, we sanctify the day, ordaining its hours as a gift from God. By doing so we give each day the kind of honor and wonder that God has intended for it and that the day deserves. As I mentioned earlier, for many years I quoted these words at the beginning of each day. I commend the practice. With this verse we set our soul's course for the day and declare ourselves on the side of God's purposes. Obviously none of us can know what any day holds when we first open our eyes upon it—or for that matter, contemplate it with our eyes still closed! But we summon faith to lay hold of the day when we settle on the divine perspective that declares, "This is the day that the LORD has made."

Not only is this a good word with which to begin the day, it is an equally good way to bring it to a close. We can speak these words in the morning by faith and in the evening in thanksgiving. Consider, too, that the mood in which we go to sleep plays a significant and sometimes crucial role in how the new day begins. However one looks at it, this is a verse—a very real, very precious promise—for the whole day: the way to begin, the place to pause at midday to reset one's course, and the way to conclude as nighttime falls.

For many years the city of Chicago had a radio personality whose key line each morning was, "It's a bee-u-ti-ful day in Chicago!" Applied to a specific city, this is old-fashioned boosterism, I suppose; but it's a kind of secular version of the biblical promise. What kind of day is this? A *perfect* day. How dare I say such a thing? Because of the Maker. What else could God make but a perfect day? When the book of Genesis tells the creation story it concludes each day's history with the signature line, "And God saw that it was good." It's as if God, the meticulous artisan, made a final check at the close of each day before closing shop and declared divine satisfaction in a task perfectly done.

My heart insists that God still does it that way. God fashions each twenty-four-hour segment with care that only that particular day could know: there is no grossness in it, no misshapen part, no margin of error. I'll go further. Since each of us is unique in having fingerprints different from the billions of others on our planet, I'll submit that each day is unique in its parts. How many days do you calculate God has made? Billions? Trillions? Who can dare to say! Have they all pleased God, giving holy joy? I believe so. I somehow feel that when the writer of Genesis portrays God as looking upon each finished day with pleasure that the writer is also suggesting that this is the way God creates each continuing day and that heaven therefore watches the day's unfolding to see what we humans will do with the unique trust God has placed in our hands.

"This is the day that the LORD has made." Here is a promise for all seasons. If the quality of the day depended on the weather, the Dow Jones average, the doctor's report, or the morning headlines, we might find it hard to see each day as perfect. But the perfection of which I speak rests in God: these are days that the *Lord* has made.

At this point I'm sure someone wants to challenge what I'm saying, or at the least to modify it. If you're thinking of a day when you will face major surgery—well, is that a perfect day? Or the day you stood in a divorce court or the day in which you received a letter or an e-mail that broke a cherished relationship: how can one see perfection in such a day? As a pastor I have walked hundreds of times on the path that leads from a funeral limousine to a place where a casket will soon be lowered: perfect? Or I've walked to my car from a home where I've learned of someone's heart-wrenching pain: perfect day?

Or you might object to my adjective on quite different grounds. It isn't the days of great sorrow or trial that distress you as much as the sameness of every day. One can cope with an occasional crisis and rise above it, but the same-old, same-old—well, that's another matter. I have sensed that issue when visiting in the continuing care section of a retirement facility. Each day in such a place, even with the best efforts at programming and menu planning, has to leave many residents feeling that tomorrow will be almost exactly the same as today. Does God make boring days too? And, if so, what's so perfect about them—or how can I cooperate with God in bringing out their perfection in my own life and in the lives of those around me?

The glory of our biblical promise is that it gives us the power to take each day captive for goodness and beauty. The quality of our days does not depend on the events they contain or promise, nor on the people with whom we live; the quality doesn't depend, even, on our health or material resources. The basic quality has already been established; these are days that the Lord God has made, and God does all things well. God makes no poor days and not even any mediocre ones. All of God's days are jewels.

It is almost certain that Jesus and his disciples sang the 118th psalm, from which this verse comes, on the night preceding his crucifixion. This passage was part of the customary ritual for the kind of service the little group of disciples had before they went out into the Mount of Olives. For Jesus, the shadow of the cross hung over the room as they sang. In a few moments they would be confronted by arresting soldiers, and before the night was past Jesus would be tried, brutalized, and sentenced to death. Yet at such a time Jesus joined his disciples in singing, "This is the day that the LORD has made."

Some years ago we Americans added a phrase to our common speech, and an acronym to make it still more operative: TGIF—"Thank God it's Friday." Perhaps you can understand that in my days as a pastor I found high irony in that popular phrase because for me Friday meant not the beginning of relaxation but the countdown toward the Sunday morning challenge of preaching. But even in these more recent years when my life has been set in the pattern of an educational institution, where Friday means a more relaxed feeling, I still have a very vigorous reaction to the TGIF philosophy. The problem, you see, is that the sentence isn't really giving thanks for Friday itself but for the fact that Friday signals an end to the other days of the week—as if Monday or Thursday were of little value. Thus, Friday is simply a day to be gotten rid of as quickly as possible in order to reach the weekend.

It's easy to live too many of our days that way. "I can hardly wait," someone says, "until vacation time," or "my wedding day," or "the trip to see our grandchildren." Worthy aims, all of them, and surely understandable. I know the feeling. But it's not a biblical way to look at life, and I doubt that it is, in the end, a wholesome outlook. Every day, after all, is a day God has made and is never therefore something to be wished away or hurried past. Who knows what wonders may be awaiting us in any given day? The day of waiting has its own splendor as much as the planned day of celebration. And sometimes the day we intended to hurry past has some unexpected wonder that makes it more memorable than the day we've designated as special.

"*This* is the day that the LORD has made." Herein is a call to live *today,* and herein is a rebuke to hurrying away any day—and also a rebuke to dreading any day. Each day has its own glory, if only we will seek to find it. Obviously the glory of some days is hidden so well that we will have to seek hard to find it—but perhaps that will make the glory of the day all the greater once its wonder is found.

So what shall we do with a perfect day, this day God has given us? If the Creator has given us such an exquisite work of art, how shall we make the most of it? Fortunately, the psalmist shows us the way—almost as if the writer wanted to be sure that we didn't lose this masterpiece by thoughtless caretaking. So here is his counsel, spoken affirmatively rather than in command: "Let us rejoice and be glad in it." A day is a precious gift and should therefore be handled with rejoicing and gladness, because this is the setting in which perfect days thrive. Pick up the new day as early as possible in the morning and study it for a few minutes. Turn it over in your soul until you begin to appreciate the delicacy of its lines, the strength of its structures. See the Creator's love woven all through it and ponder anew: God has been making days farther back than any measure of calendar or science can estimate and hasn't tired of it yet. God must surely take satisfaction in the making of days, to continue doing so without tedium, and surely God must find that special satisfaction all artists experience when they see their work appreciated by those who benefit from it.

So take the day with gladness and rejoicing. It is a perfect thing, delivered with love. Give thanks to the One who made it, and dedicate all its loveliness in the spirit of its Maker. Two things are especially important in this process. First, gladness, because gladness sets the theme for the day. And then, rejoicing, because rejoicing is the very heartbeat of God's creation. A day thrives on rejoicing as a baby thrives on love. And, of course, dedicate the day to the God who gave it, because in doing so we are putting the day into the hands of the one who knows best how to bring this day and every day to its ultimate purposes.

And I should also add a word of precaution. I've made mention of how to handle this day in the morning hour, but that can sometimes be a little late. The Hebrew Scriptures taught that a new day begins not with the morning's sunrise but in the previous evening's sunset; thus, it is that observant Jews begin their Sabbath on Friday evening rather than Saturday morning. There's a good deal of spiritual wisdom in this practice. Many a new day is half lost by the burden of worry, resentment, or recrimination that we take to bed with us the night before. Monday morning gets its direction on Sunday night. Give thanks to God for the new day as you dedicate yourself to sleep, so God can purge your mind, your nerves, your memory, your spirit. Thus these elements of our nature will be in working order for the hour of rising, enabling us to capture morning with rejoicing and gladness.

From the Garden of Eden through the parables of Jesus, the Bible describes you and me as *stewards,* persons entrusted by God with all sorts of potential. We are stewards of God's creation, of human relationships, of our own individual potential before God.

And eventually the issue comes down to our being stewards of each day—most especially the one in which we are now engaged. Next to our eternal souls, this day is our highest trust from God: higher, even, than our abilities, our personalities, our influence, and our possessions. Because all the rest of what has been entrusted to our stewardship has its scene of action in the course of this day. Indeed, our handling of this day shapes the very contours of our souls.

As I realize that unnerving fact, I take strength in knowing from whence this day has come: it is a day the Lord has made, and the Lord has made it perfectly. And I take further strength in knowing that there is a formula for fulfilling the potential and perfection that this day holds: "Let us rejoice and be glad in it."

That's promise enough for any day! It's the kind of promise that will keep us every day.

CHAPTER 4

THE WORLD IN GOD'S EMBRACE

For God so loved the world, that he gave his only begotten
Son, that whosoever believeth in him should not perish, but
have everlasting life. (John 3:16 KJV)

If I were an artist, I would never attempt a sunset. I know it would be too much for me, that I simply could not catch enough of it to satisfy myself, or you either. If anyone asked me to put a sunset on canvas, I'd have to reply, "Go view the original for yourself. Whatever I do will only diminish your experience."

I am not an artist but a preacher, a teacher, and a writer; however, I've chosen just now to put myself in a sunset situation. There are some verses in the Bible that have such a sunset quality that one ventures on the impossible by trying to explain or enlarge them. But since I've spent most of my life trying to do the impossible—that is, to open the Scriptures of the Old and New Testament by preaching, teaching, and writing—I have no right to excuse myself from discussing a Bible verse that nearly all of us count among our favorites: John 3:16. It's quite possible that you assumed this verse would have a place in a book of the Bible's great promises—and you have a right to feel I've sold my assignment short if I don't discuss it with you. So I make this caveat, that I know I can't do the verse justice—and now I charge ahead!

I think of two preachers a generation ago who were comparing feelings as to their favorite verses of Scripture. "John three sixteen," the one man said promptly.

"No," the other answered, "that's not fair. John three sixteen isn't a verse of the Bible; it's the whole book."

Martin Luther said the same thing when he interpreted this verse for the last time, just a fortnight before his death. "What Spartan saying can be compared with this wonderful brevity?" he asked. "It is a Bible in itself." In his dying moments Luther repeated this verse three times in Latin, the language in which he had first known the Bible. Can you think of a better word with which to die?

But all of us have a problem with this verse. It is not only the incomprehensible majesty of it or its grand sweep and its indifference to all of our ordinary boundaries of thought and perception. Ironically, it is its familiarity. It is like the Lord's Prayer and Psalm twenty-three—it is one of those passages that many of us learned without knowing we had learned it, or learned so long ago that we can't remember when first it became part of our faith vocabulary. For sixteen years I was the minister of a church with a grand carillon. The bells rang out every fifteen minutes, from morning till evening, with some of the most exquisite sound one could imagine. But because my office was in the church, where I could hear the sound day after day, several thousand times a year, it came to be that much of the time I didn't hear them at all. I had allowed their glory and majesty to become common and at last unheard. So it is with this magnificent body of words from the Scriptures: "For God so loved the world, that he gave his only begotten Son, that whosoever believeth in him should not perish, but have everlasting life" (KJV).

Because the promise is so big it is probably best for me to take it apart word by word to see if in the process we can catch some new glimpse of its wonder. The verse begins as sentences so often do, with a subject—and the subject is God: *For God*. In this, it reminds us of the opening words of the Bible in the book of Genesis: *In the beginning God* (Genesis 1:1 KJV). It is wonderfully appropriate that the key statement about our human race begins with the same ultimate noun as the declaration about the created nature of our universe. The story of our universe begins with God, and the status of the key inhabitant of this universe—as we know it—begins with God. Genesis portrays God as the key element in our universe (and thus of its ultimate character), and John 3:16 identifies God as the defining fact of our standing and prospect as human creatures.

So God is the noun. But now the big issue: what is the verb? Because the verb—what God does or says or thinks—is going to reveal what kind of God God is. The verb makes all the difference. The verb reveals God in action, and thus the verb reveals the character of God. And the verb is *loves*. God loves.

Most of humankind's religions speak of humans seeking God, portraying gods who are out-of-reach. Indeed, typically these religions perceive gods who must be placated or bought off. The Christian gospel declares a quite astonishing thing: that God not only responds to us but that God's defining response is love. "For God so loved . . ."

This leads us to the other basic element in the sentence, the object of the verb. What, then, shall God love? We are known by the loves we keep. For some, the object of love is power or possessions or, quite simply, self. And at our best, love shows judgment—or as some would put it, taste. We love what is beautiful, appealing, worthy. And it is just here that the love of God shocks us. God's love is disturbingly indiscriminating. A sophisticate might say that God has no taste. Because, you see, God loves *the world*.

This remarkable verse gives us no adjective. It doesn't say what kind of world God loves or what portions of the world. We will see as the verse unfolds that "the world" is referring to the earth's human inhabitants. One doesn't have to live very long before one discovers that earth's inhabitants are a very mixed breed. We are lovable and we are courting of hate, we are admirable and we are despicable, we are beautiful and we are crude, we are kind and generous and we are brutally selfish. And come to think of it, it's not only that these are the varieties of people in the world, it is also true that from time to time some variation of these qualities appears in all of us as individuals.

But God loves this world regardless. God's love is not limited to the worthy—though some of us think it should be that way in those times when we think ourselves to be admirable. Nor does God love only the pure and the lovable. God's love is utterly without discrimination. God embraces the whole, disparate, chaotic mass and mess of our human race. And God does so in the divine expectation that such love will transform our human race, person by person.

Still, some questions remain. All of us know by experience that love can be a very nominal thing. It can be earnestly spoken, especially in surges of feeling, then lived out quite indifferently until it means almost nothing. You remember that when Eliza Dolittle's sentimental young lover in the musical "My Fair Lady" sings of his love for her, Eliza explodes that she's "so sick of words." Love had better *do* something. If love is no more than a word it is a kind of blasphemy. By its definition, love ought to *do,* it ought to find living expression. So what does God do when God loves? Is love just another word in the divine vocabulary, or does it amount to something? Is love active?

The grand promise doesn't leave us in doubt. "For God so loved the world that he *gave...*" God is a giving God. Martin Luther used to tell a strange and wonderful little story about a printer's daughter in Germany. Her father was printing Luther's translation of the Bible. Pieces of his work would, of course, often fall to the floor of his shop. One day the little girl picked up a scrap of paper on which she found just the words, "God so loved the world that he gave." This was a revelation to her, nearly unbelievable. Until then she had always been told that the Almighty was to be feared and that he could be approached only through acts of penance. The radiance in her life was suddenly so obvious that her mother inquired the reason. The girl handed her mother the crumpled piece of paper with the unfinished sentence. The mother was perplexed: "He gave—but what was it he gave?" The girl hesitated for only a moment, then said, "I don't know; but if he loved us well enough to give us anything, we need not be afraid of him."

The girl's instinct was true and certain. But a question still remains. Let me put it by recasting a common phrase: "What does a God give who has everything?" That is, since God has such abundance, is there any truly costly gift? Those of us who live with average means sometimes are put off by stories of what the very rich are giving for Christmas. Perhaps instead we should feel sorry for them. When you have untold millions, how do you give something that really, *really* costs you something?

So what does God give? Anything that comes to mind seems trivial in the light of God's abundance. If, as the psalmist says, the cattle on a thousand hills are God's, and if all the minerals in the bowels of the earth—including some minerals that we haven't yet discovered or haven't learned how to put to use—what then can God give that shows any real goodness in the divine Heart? So I repeat: what does a God give who has everything? What can God give that has some significance, some worthy measure of love?

This promise tells the answer. God gave his Son. And the King James Version makes the point with appropriate poignancy: the *only begotten son*. This gift is irreplaceable; there is no other like it. In this gift, God gives of his very self. God has everything, so that any imaginable gift would be an indifferent dent in the vast resources. Diamonds, perhaps, or some other mineral deposit? Or a planet? God has not only an abundant supply but also the time to allow for the production of more diamonds or what have you. But God has only one Son. There is none other like him, and nothing can take his place. If a God who has everything is to demonstrate love by giving, the God of the Scriptures has done just that in giving the only gift that cannot be replaced, the only gift that will *hurt*: the only begotten Son.

Now what is the purpose of all this? What will God achieve with such loving? Here we are introduced to God's grand dream: "that whosoever believeth in him should not perish, but have everlasting life." God intends by this gift to bring salvation to our human race.

Let me tell you what I know about this gift and its results, as I have observed it in my own life and in our world. At a personal level, let this be said. When we feel unloved and unlovable—a not uncommon experience, because there are times when others reject us, making us feel unloved, and times when for reasons sometimes hard to explain, we reject ourselves—one can take hold of this good word. If God so loves us that the only begotten Son has been given in our behalf, then our worth (our lovableness, so to speak) must be greater than we realized. Who are we to discredit ourselves, or who is in a position to discredit us, if God finds us so supremely attractive and so ultimately valuable? Take heart, weary soul! Your value is greater than you can realize.

I remind myself of this verse on those occasions when I cross paths (even if only in the newspapers) with persons who seem to me to be utterly unlovable—the kind of persons who seem to us to be of no value, whose only worth seems to be in bringing down the general pattern of worth for our human race. I must treat each person with regard and respect because he or she is someone for whom Christ died. So what if that person's style is unattractive to me, or if I find his or her conduct repugnant? So what if that person irritates my sensibilities or falls outside my boundaries of respectability? I am under the reign of One who loves these persons so much, and who sees such innate value in them, that his only Son dies for their redemption. How dare I treat with scorn one for whom Christ died?

And when I look at this promise, I need to extend my

vision beyond individuals to look at the wider world in which we live. If "God so loved the *world*," then the promise is a corporate one as well as one expressed in individuals. I rejoice in that knowledge, even as I am convicted by it. Our world seems sometimes to be so perverse. We blame it sometimes on the media, but the media quickly replies that it is simply reflecting the times. We answer that this culture does not reflect us or the people we know. Sometimes we're inclined to think that the whole world has gone mad and that only we and a few people we know are keeping their moorings.

Well, we're not the first to feel that way. I suspect this was the mood of the psalmist twenty-five or thirty centuries ago when he felt that he was "an alien in Meshech," because "I am for peace; / but when I speak, / they are for war" (Psalm 120:5, 7). Martin Luther felt that the world was out of joint in his time. "If I were as our Lord God," he said, "...and these vile people were as disobedient as they now be, I would break the world in pieces." It seems so often as if our human race is irrational, stupidly dedicated to its own destruction—individually, in institutions, in nations. When I would despair in my analysis of the times in which we live, or when I read or hear such views from a theologian or a political analyst, I have to remind myself that God still loves this world. God has invested in it so heavily, by way of his Son, that I must rededicate myself to the purposes of God in seeking to redeem this world.

"For God so loved the world." If that be true, is anyone out of the reach of this divine embrace? Dare I give up on any individual? Is anyone so hateful, so bewildered, so resentful or confused that the arms of God's love cannot bring him or her in? How wide is God's embrace? And the promise answers, "As wide as the world." Wide enough to reach the most self-justifying Pharisee, the angriest hater of humankind, the most arrogant denier of God, the one most despising of himself: God's love embraces all—and God's Spirit searches for all.

Almost a century ago a relatively unknown poet and composer, Frederick M. Lehman, put together words and a tune of his own to extol the love of God. I suspect that the language and the figures of speech are a touch too predictable to be good poetry. But he has it right when he summarizes the love of God with a reach from the Garden of Eden to eternity. The concluding verse of the hymn reaches to the limits:

> "Could we with ink the oceans fill, And were the skies of
>   parchment made,
> Were every stalk on earth a quill, And ev'ry man a scribe by
>   trade;
> To write the love of God above Would drain the ocean dry;
> Nor could the scroll contain the whole, Tho' stretched from
>   sky to sky.[1]

A footnote in an old hymnbook reports that this stanza was penciled on the wall of a narrow room of an asylum by a man said to have been demented and that the lines were discovered after his death. Obviously, I can't verify the story, and I surely would not deny it. In truth some of literature's greatest poetry has been written by persons in the midst of mental, spiritual, or emotional turmoil, some of it in times of hospitalization and even of incarceration. And I am particularly sure that the love of God would not only be real under such circumstances; more than that, God's love would have a new depth of reality and of irrefutability.

Because if ever the love of God shows itself to be our planet's ultimate reality, it is when some person has reached the end of the rope. Then, when we can no longer hold on, the love of God holds us. This I want to affirm. Here is a promise that will keep us.

NOTE

1. Frederick M. Lehman, "The Love of God," *Favorite Hymns of Praise* (Chicago: Tabernacle Publishing Company, 1972), 166.

CHAPTER 5

MERCY FOR OUR POOREST DAYS

A bruised reed shall he not break, and smoking flax shall he not quench. (Matthew 12:20 KJV)

The biblical promises that mean the most to us are those that we *own.* They are the verses that become our particular possession because in some way or at some time their messages have been uniquely appropriate and thus the verses themselves have become uniquely our own. Sometimes we own a verse because of what it has meant to a friend or family member, and we possess it by spiritual inheritance. For a person outside the community or faith this sense of personal possession may seem quite arrogant: how dare one claim that some verse of the Bible is peculiarly one's own? Does God or one of God's angels spend time assigning Bible verses to mere mortals? But for the person in some valley of a shadow, it is a matter not of one's special importance but of one's special need.

I was sixteen years old when the verse before us became mine. Something was bothering me at the time. I can't imagine now what it would have been. I was in the first semester of my senior year in high school, and in many respects the world was my oyster. True, we were very poor,

but so were most of my friends, so poverty wasn't a defining issue. Besides, I had a morning paper route, and although that meant arising at 4:30 each morning, seven days
a week, it also meant I could buy a Coney Island hot dog
after a school game. I was president of a high school liter-
ary society, vice president of my class, had a weekly sports
radio broadcast on one of our city's two radio stations—for
my small world, life was good.

But you may remember that when one is sixteen, the
human ego is especially fragile and unpredictable. And
what's worse, when you're a teenager you haven't yet lived
long enough to know the wisdom of that adage, "This, too,
shall pass." You think you'll be downcast forever.

So, yes, I was a troubled young man: something in my
psyche felt rejected and worthless, and since I couldn't put
my finger on the reason, the despondency grew all the
worse. It was then that a wise woman who had been a
teacher and a counselor to me—not by official position but
simply by virtue of her godliness and her concern for me—
offered a memorable word. "Remember the promise,
Ellsworth," she said, "A bruised reed shall he not break, and
smoking flax shall he not quench, till he send forth judgment unto victory." Since then, I have quoted that verse
hundreds of times, often to myself and many times to
downcast souls who have come my way.

This verse appears in both the Old and New Testaments. Originally it was part of a promise from the prophet
Isaiah who assured his nation that someday there would
come to them a benevolent ruler who would govern with
kindness, mercy, and justice. Six or seven centuries later,
the writer of the Gospel of Matthew saw these words fulfilled in Jesus of Nazareth and quoted them in his story of
the life and teachings of our Lord.

The few words contain two interesting figures of
speech. The reed is a lovely plant but altogether commonplace in the part of the world from which the Bible has
come. It flourishes by the sides of almost any river and in

marshes and standing waters. People sometimes used it to decorate their homes, and the stems were convenient as a measuring device, a kind of homemade ruler or yardstick, so to speak. You may remember that when the soldiers were mocking Jesus shortly before his crucifixion that they put a reed in his hand as a burlesque of a king's scepter. It was a clever touch, even if a heartless and somewhat clumsy one. The flax was made into linen, of course, but in this verse it is referred to in its other ancient household use, as a wick for the common lamp.

So see what the verse is saying? The reed is commonplace, of some little value as long as it retains its form and shape and some degree of strength. But what good is a *bruised* reed? Obviously it is something then to be cast aside, useless. The flax is valuable when its texture is such that it makes a good lamp wick. But suppose it is a bit thick or moist so that instead of shedding a steady, dependable light it only smokes and smolders. Now it is worse than useless; throw it away!

The issue in the figure of speech is, of course, persons. What shall be done with those persons who are like the reed, worthy enough if all goes well, but commonplace at best—and then, one day, they're bruised. When bruised they are quite useless; they can make no contribution to the general welfare and indeed are likely to be a burden. And the flax: if it can't perform the function for which it has worth—if, indeed, it smokes and discolors rather than providing brightness—what, then, shall we do with it? Our world has a pretty well-established pattern, varying according to the temperament of the individual or the institution. Those who are brutal stomp on the bruised reed and smoking flax; failure and uselessness are offensive to them. Others, more civilized, are nevertheless uneasy around bruised reed and smoking flax. We wouldn't discard them but neither do we want to be around them. People who have dealt with a life-threatening malignancy or perhaps a divorce or some embarrassing family crisis report that many friends break contact—and the friends explain that they "aren't comfortable" around the bruised one and that they don't know what to say, so they simply break off communication.

But I must also speak a word of praise. Over the years I have been impressed with how many people care about the human soul who is bruised or broken. I am especially impressed with those who work in institutions where they spend their hours each day tending the hopelessly invalid or the severely limited or the mentally or socially limited. Indeed, I venture that the best measure of the quality of a civilization is shown in its concern for and its care of the bruised reed and the smoking flax. What do we do with those who are least able to defend themselves, those with little to commend them, perhaps little to make them attractive or winsome? In some cases part of the person's problem is that they are socially difficult, exhausting the persons who might extend help. When we seek to relate to such human need we need, indeed, the spirit of Christ: "A broken reed shall he not break, and smoking flax shall he not quench."

The gracious promises of God turn out sometimes to be God's commands. If God shows mercy to the flax and reed, then we who claim to follow God are under command to do the same. If we have received mercy, we can do no less than extend it to others. I am proud that the world's great systems of mercy—hospitals, institutions caring for the aged, the helpless, the forsaken, the orphaned—began with the biblical faith. Government and secular charities came to these concerns relatively lately. But whatever pride we might feel in the church's involvement is tempered by the realization that we should do so much more. And yes, more: we must confess that we are simply paying a debt; we have received mercy, so we must give it. We have known ourselves to be bruised reed and smoking flax, so how can we do other than to help those who are now in such need?

Consider how much of Jesus' time was given to the

bruised reed and the smoking flax. One thinks of his feeding the multitudes. The disciples had said, "Send them home," but Jesus replied, "They have been with us several days and it is a long journey." He gave his time to the bruised and the faltering and spent his emotional and spiritual energy tending to their brokenness. When children were brought to Jesus, some in the crowd felt that a teacher should not be interrupted for children, but Jesus took them to himself and blessed them. Women were second-class citizens in that first-century world, but Jesus gave them primary significance by the attention he paid to them. Certain diseases—especially leprosy—isolated people, and most sicknesses were seen as evidences of divine judgment. Jesus, however, reached out to touch the lepers—the very symbol of the untouchable. He healed every kind of sickness and brought deliverance to the persons whose mental states terrified others. Certain classes of people, such as the tax collectors and public sinners, were despised as outsiders; Jesus chose to eat and socialize with them.

And above all, Jesus nurtured the faint flame of spiritual life. No part of our human structure is more delicate, more susceptible to both good and ill, than our spirit. At one moment it can be ready to march into the face of death and not much later stumble at the sight of a gnat. We think of Simon Peter, such a vigorous, dramatic, and outspoken soul, so ready to declare his allegiance and at times also to belittle his comrades. But he could also, just as easily, cower off in confusion. He had told Jesus he would never forsake him—all of the others might do so, Peter said, but not he. And as you know he denied Jesus three times within a matter of hours and did so finally with an oath.

Now the bruised reed was surely broken, the smoking flax extinguished. But after Jesus' resurrection an angelic messenger told the women at the tomb that they should tell Jesus' disciples *and Peter* that Jesus was risen, so they could meet him in Galilee (Mark 16:7). Simon Peter got a singular invitation because he was singularly bruised and nearly broken. Jesus was about to restore the bruised reed, to bring new value to the smoking flax.

I once knew a man who seemed to have so much going for him. He was a man of faith and of earnest character. But as he allowed the troubles and distresses of his life to become larger than the promises of God, he lost heart; and as he lost heart, his life began to disintegrate. Finally, it seemed as if all were lost—his career, his personal life, his reputation, his hopes and dreams. Then somehow, some way, he received a message of hope: his life was bruised, but God would not break him nor would God allow him to be broken even if it seemed that he deserved such breaking. His wick of life was smoldering, but God would not quench it in disgust. Instead, God reached to the man and began gently to nurture the bruised reed, then to blow quietly on the smoking flax until at last the man was restored, restored. This is a marvel and a miracle, but it happens so often, because our Lord will not break the bruised reed or quench the smoking flax.

Long ago I knew a Hollywood musician whose career was destroyed by alcohol. He had been the accompanist and arranger for two of the most popular vocalists of the period. I met him the night he turned to Christ for salvation. He was converted and transformed, no doubt about it. But one day he slipped, fell off into a long period of drunkenness. What a bruised reed he became! Then he sent word that he wanted to try again; he would be returning to town on a Greyhound bus. I can still visualize that Greyhound station as he stepped off the bus—so ashamed, so defeated, so bruised and lost. But God received him again, and he was restored. His greatest and happiest and most fruitful years followed.

At quite another venue, I think of an aged woman in a nursing home. In her long and vigorous prime she had been so proud and self-sufficient, delightful in her scorn of weakness. Now she was helpless. "I'm only a burden to everyone," she wept. But God did not break this bruised reed;

God nurtured the beauty that still lay deep in her life and brought forth new elements of beauty that no one could have imagined in the strong woman they had known earlier. One of my favorite bruised reeds is the Anglican rector Geoffrey Studdert-Kennedy, who all but stumbled into fame as a chaplain during World War I when he became known to thousands of British soldiers as "Woodbine Willie." It is clear that he battled fiercely with his own twists of personality and his own ravaged body. But more than that, he chose through all of his ministry to fight on the side of causes where the odds were exceedingly long, and to pour his energy into people and issues that could hardly be expected to survive. Not only was he himself a bruised reed, he allied himself with bruised reeds and smoking flax.

Recently, in a curious moment, I checked my copy of *Oxford Dictionary of Quotations* to see if this verse might be there. I didn't expect it to be. After all, there are thousands of Bible verses from which the compilers of a book of quotations would select the most memorable hundreds. I did not expect it to be in the *Oxford* and checked only to confirm my expectations. But it was there! And when I looked, then, in the other standard source, *Bartlett's Familiar Quotations,* it was there too.

Why? Quite simply, because no experience in human life is more common than that of the bruised reed and the smoking flax. If there is any word that needs to be spoken at youth, at middle age, or in life's decrepitude, it is this: God will not break the bruised reed or quench the smoking flax.

The incomparable John Milton learned this about as dramatically as anyone. At age forty-four, with his talent apparently at its best, Milton's career as scholar and poet seemed about to end with oncoming blindness. Several years later he poured out his agony in words that are now familiar to millions:

When I consider how my light is spent
   'Ere half my days in this dark world and wide
   And that one talent which is death to hide,
Lodged with me useless…

At this point Milton raises the question, would "God, re-turning, chide?" Fortunately Milton had the faith to know better. He concluded that "who best / Bear his mild yoke, they serve him best. / They also serve who only stand and wait."

As it happens, Milton's most remarkable work was still ahead. Not only was his gift not left with him useless, he would go on to write "Paradise Lost" and "Paradise Regained."

Because, you see, the mercy of Christ is more than pity, more even than divine compassion. Mind you, all of us have known days when pity itself is a good and necessary gift, particularly if we feel despised and hopeless. But pity alone can be debilitating—a good place to visit, but not a place to set up an emotional home.

So remember the rest of this grand promise. "A bruised reed shall he not break, and smoking flax shall he not quench, *till he send forth judgment unto victory*." Christ will win! Gentle as is his method, he will win. Our Lord takes upon himself the burden of human defeat, the lost causes of humanity, the bruised reeds and the smoking flax, the motley days of our lives —and with such stuff, Christ wins! And he will not stop "until he brings justice to victory" (Matthew 12:20).

As for that sixteen-year-old boy who claimed this verse as his own so long ago: he lived through that difficult time, whatever it was. And he has lived through several since then. Sometimes, truth be told, with daily frequency. And always he finds it true: there is mercy for the bruised reed and the smoking flax, until our Lord brings forth justice into victory. You can count on it. This is a promise that will hold you.

44

CHAPTER 6

LIVING IN THE SUNLIGHT

[handwritten annotations: unwilling to feel remorse + repent / apostasy / revolt from God]

There is therefore now no condemnation for those who are in Christ Jesus. (Romans 8:1)

At your first reading you may conclude that there is little need for this promise at this point in the cultural history of the Western world. We are residents of the feel-good age. It has been our emotional abode for roughly a full generation. We work overtime at telling our children how able, how beautiful, how winsome they are because we want to be sure they have a good self-image. At the end of the grade school athletic season we present awards not only to the first, second, and third place winners but to everyone—simply for having competed. We want to be sure that no one feels like a loser.

But deep inside, we know it doesn't quite work. If we're present when the everyone-gets-one awards are given, we know that the adults supervising the occasion—all of them losers—sense that they are only postponing the inevitable for the children. Eventually all of us have to suffer defeat, and with it some kind of condemnation. Some of this condemnation comes from without—from people and institutions and expectations that condemn us. But much, perhaps most, comes from within. And it comes from within, ironically, because we want to be better than we are.

Something in us, in one form or another, makes us see a higher goal and desire it—and not reaching it, we feel condemnation.

Now, in truth, a certain kind of self-judgment and the commensurate self-condemnation is good. If there is any progress for our human race it comes because some individual or some group wants to improve. The reason poetry has gotten beyond doggerel and the automobile beyond a wagon is because someone was striving for improvement. And especially, ultimately, the reason the saint has gotten beyond most of us faltering, fumbling humans is because of such striving. Such striving comes from discontent, and discontent includes an element of condemnation. So condemnation, in itself, is not bad. It's what we do with it that produces debilitating mental and spiritual anguish.

Most of us have had some experience with that kind of self-condemnation. For some it is a way station toward a better life, but for others it is a constant struggle and a terribly self-defeating one at that. This latter group knows Condemnation with a capital C, a body of death to be carried about every day.

That grand theologian, that first miracle convert to Christianity, that restless philosopher, the Apostle Paul understood self-condemnation. He knew the hidden wonder of its potential, but he knew even more clearly the hell of its anguish. And it is Paul who assures us that it is possible to live in the sunlight. He shows us how to direct life's struggle toward self-enhancement rather than toward self-destruction.

But before we begin visiting with Paul, let me face a question that is almost certainly on your mind. It's popular to say that religion in general, and Christianity in particular, is responsible for our feelings of self-condemnation. Thus, Karl Marx wrote, "The first requisite for the happiness of the people is the abolition of religion."[1] H. L. Mencken, certainly one of the most popular journalists of his time, made something of the same point when he defined Puritanism:

"The haunting fear that someone, somewhere, may be happy."² A type, perhaps a perversion, of psychology insists that religion imposes a sense of guilt on people, so that it is impossible for them to be happy.

Well, let's be honest about it: some people have this kind of religion, and some preachers encourage it. And from what I have observed, some people seem by nature to look for this kind of religion. There isn't time here to discuss the matter fully, but most of us have known persons who seem in some perverse fashion to find pleasure in misery. They seek ways to belittle themselves, and while they may also seek to impose this attitude on others, the main object of their condemnation is their own person.

In truth, we have a bit of a moral conundrum. At our best, we humans want to be better. The greatest souls have always had some measure of restlessness, some feeling that they ought to be better than they are. I suspect that the persons who have made the greatest contributions to human progress and to human happiness are persons who have been driven by just such a sense. And a fair amount of that outlook rests in every human soul. We can be done with it by constantly selling ourselves out to evil or to evil's younger brother, mediocrity, but for most of us the urge to excellence whips us on.

And so, ironically, the potential for self-condemnation seems written into our psyches. Some preacher or moralist or poet may press it upon us still further, but the potential is there in the deepest recesses of our souls. The standards may vary between times and peoples, so that the morals of one society may be only the mores of another. But the quality of accountability is written into all of society, always and everywhere. That's the difference between being human and being ape, the difference between Thomas and tomcat.

It's quite astonishing how this sense of condemnation pursues us. Sheldon Vanauken recalls what he later realized was the beginning of the turning point in the life of his wife,

Davy. While he was a graduate student at Yale he left her one evening happily curled in a chair reading a book. When he came home later that evening, she was weeping desperately. "Her sins, she said, had come out and paraded before her, ghastly in appearance and mocking in demeanour." Recalling that evening Sheldon asks, "What sins? What sins could this eager, loving creature have committed? Not sins as the world counts sins. Not one person had she murdered, nor one gold ingot stolen. No unfaithfulness, no secret drinking, no dishonesty, no sloth, no kicking dogs." Then he continues, "Sin: she knew there was such a thing as plain sin, not something any psychiatrist could absolve or explain away."[3]

Two things stand out in Davy Vanauken's experience. First, she was not a really bad person. There was no monstrous wickedness in her—actually, almost the opposite. But this sense of condemnation, you see, has to do not so much with the evil we have done as with the gap between our potential and our doing. Thus, a relatively good person will sometimes feel more sense of condemnation than a careless one, just as a concert pianist or violinist will be jarred by a minor dissonance that the rest of us don't even hear.

Second, I am captured by Vanauken's statement that this sense of sin was something that could not by human means be absolved or explained away. All of us have our daily devices for dealing with this issue. We point to other people whom we judge to be worse, or we work out a gradation of sin in which our conduct is rated relatively harmless. Thus, the car thief says that what he does is nothing compared to the rip-off by certain politicians, and the call girl compares herself favorably with the suburban wife who's carrying on an affair with her husband's colleague.

But in time all such reasoning is of no avail. We may think that such arguments convince others, and perhaps they do—or more likely, they give others some ammunition for dealing with their own similar problems. We may think we have convinced ourselves, though usually, as Shakespeare put it, "The lady doth protest too much, methinks." We don't really fool ourselves. Not for long, if at all. Even those of us who become most hardened to sin are only pushing the guilt down where it can eat away at our psyche or—perhaps worse yet—where we desensitize our judgment so that we have less and less ability to distinguish between the real and the counterfeit, the shoddy and the beautiful.

This self-condemnation has something to do with our human conscience. As such, it is not entirely dependable, because the conscience—though basically, it seems to me, a divine gift—is powerfully influenced by our circumstances, our culture, and our upbringing. But the instinct for self-condemnation goes deeper. It is part of our genetic code, and it is so deeply implanted that it demands more than some passing nostrum. It must be dealt with, no doubt about it.

So I come back to the Apostle Paul and to his great, sublimely hopeful promise: "There is therefore now no condemnation for those who are in Christ Jesus." Paul's testimony deserves hearing, because he knew the problem at first hand. Paul was the kind of meticulous soul who was not content with any imperfection in himself. It was this kind of scrupulosity that drove Paul to membership in the Pharisees, the most demanding religious sect of his day, or perhaps of any day. He tells us of the soul-anguish with which he had come to live. "I am a creature of flesh and blood," he explained. "I cannot understand what I do. What I want to do, that I do not do; but what I hate, that I do" (Romans 7:15, Barclay). At last he cries out, "O wretched man that I am! Who will deliver me from this fatal body?" (Romans 7:24, Barclay).

Then Paul answers his own question with a grand shout. "God will!" But how does God do so? "There is therefore now no condemnation for those who are in Christ Jesus." The key word is *now,* and the key phrase is *in Christ*

Jesus. Paul is telling us that a change has come in the human story. He is reciting not simply his own experience but a fact that includes the whole human race, for all who will receive it. There is a difference between *then* and *now*. *Then,* before Christ, there was no really adequate or effective way to deal with human condemnation; *now,* now that Christ has come, there is. Before Christ, Paul explains, the Jews had a magnificent gift in the Law. (He could have added, from his own studies, that the Greeks and also the Romans had a worthy gift in their strenuously developed philosophy.) But the Law of the Hebrew Torah could only document our failings; it couldn't save us from them. And the Roman poet Ovid, who died while Paul was still a boy, could only say, "I see the better things, and I approve them, but I follow the worse,"[4] which is much like Paul's own experience as described in Romans 7:15. Thus the Hebrew Law and the secular philosophers seemed only to intensify our human problem. They gave us a mirror that made it easier for us to see our moral failing—and this, mind you, is a gift in its own right—but offered no power to heal or redeem us.

But *now,* Paul insists, we have a different scenario. A new opportunity has opened before us: we can live *"in Christ Jesus."* The basic case for self-condemnation may be as great as ever and so also the reasons for feeling condemned, but we no longer have to live in that neighborhood. We might say, in the style of John Bunyan, that we once lived in a city called Condemnation, but that now we have moved into a new community, a city call Salvation—salvation in Jesus Christ. There is a special dramatic quality in that little preposition *in.* If we are only *near* Christ Jesus we might still be in danger, but we are privileged to be *in* him, secure from any attacks hell might make.

Paul makes his case in the language of the courtroom. The Greek word our Bible translates "condemnation" was a legal term in Paul's day, referring to the punishment that followed sentencing. In that vein Paul explains that we humans are under sentence of law, the law of sin and death. But a new law has taken effect, the law of the Spirit, which brings life in Jesus Christ. Thus, the old law of sin and death has been nullified by the new law of life in Christ.

But how, exactly, did Jesus break the power of sin and death? Paul explains, by becoming a "sin offering with that very same human nature which in us had sinned" (Romans 8:3, Barclay). That is, Jesus came in a human body so that he might take the penalty of sin and die as a "sin offering." Paul was using the language and concept he had known from his upbringing in the Hebrew Law, where animals were sacrificed to pay the penalty for sin. Paul explains that Jesus had come to be just such a sin offering for the human race. And by his death, Jesus "condemned sin" so that it no longer has power over those who accept what Christ has done. Thus, we are no longer condemned because *sin* has been condemned, and its reign and dominance has been broken.

Charles Wesley, the co-founder of the Methodist movement and a songwriter for all of Christendom, related his own spiritual journey in many of his hymns. Like Paul, he knew a good deal about self-condemnation, and like Paul he had tried being a Pharisee—in his case, in the Holy Club he started in his days at Oxford. But on the first anniversary of his conversion to a wonderfully vibrant faith, Wesley wrote,

> He [Christ] breaks the power of cancelled sin,
> He sets the prisoner free;
> His blood can make the foulest clean;
> His blood availed for me.[5]

Wesley affirmed a kind of double assurance: the power of sin had been *cancelled,* and Christ proceeded further to *break* it. No wonder, then, that the prisoner is "set free"!

We must, of course, act on God's goodness. It is not that we can now do whatever we please because condemnation has been lifted. Rather, we now possess the inclination and the power to live a different kind of life. We are not above falling, but we have new strength to rise again and we know where to find our help. By God's grace we have a new ability—a divine ability—to live triumphantly.

The best news in this whole story is the realization that God is on our side. If we feel condemned, we have to know that our sense of condemnation is not from God. God, after all, has sought to break the power of sin and the condemnation that it brings by the gift of Jesus Christ. The condemnation, therefore, cannot be from God if we have accepted God's gracious offer. Any condemnation we feel is either of our own making or the subtle but debilitating suggestion of hell. That suggestion may come from the culture in which we live or from a certain kind of admonition from friends or parents or preachers. But remember always that preaching that brings condemnation but that does not lead on to the grace of forgiveness in Christ is not Christian preaching.

The Apostle Paul had found a solid foundation for his soul. He could face the fact that he had fallen short—a reality which it is foolish and unproductive to deny. But he had learned not to take up residence in his failures or his weakness. Having confessed his sins to God and having committed himself to a new way of life, he declared himself free of condemnation, because he was now in Christ Jesus.

This is good news for all of us. It is good news for the alcoholic when everybody seems to have given up on him. It's good news for the man who fears that his glands are stronger than he is. It's good news for the woman who fears she can never stop hating a person who has wronged her. And it's good news for the rather average Christian who tries earnestly to live a better life but feels condemned for her poor human slips and failures.

The promise is sure and absolute. "There is therefore *now* [since the change that has come] *no* condemnation

What does this mean?

[none whatsoever] for those who are *in Christ Jesus* [an utterly safe dwelling place for the soul]." *convict*
There will always be persons who will condemn us, including well-meaning persons—and often enough they will be able to make a strong case. There will be frequent times when we will condemn ourselves—for some, more often than condemnation from others. But there is a secure spiritual ground to which we can go: the place bought for us by the One who has taken upon himself the sins of the world—and who in doing so has promised a better way of living for all who will trust in him. "There is therefore no condemnation to those who are in Christ Jesus, who walk not after the flesh but after the Spirit." This is a promise that will keep you, no matter the thieves who would steal it away.

NOTES

1. Joseph L. Boron, ed., *A Treasury of Jewish Quotations* (South Brunswick, N.J.: Thomas Yoseloff, 1965), 405.
2. Elizabeth Knowles, ed., *Oxford Dictionary of Quotations*, 6th edition (New York: Oxford University Press, 2004), 521.
3. Sheldon Vanauken, *A Severe Mercy* (San Francisco: Harper & Row, 1977), 67-68.
4. Elizabeth Knowles, ed., *Oxford Dictionary of Quotations*, 6th edition (New York: Oxford University Press, 2004), 580.
5. Charles Wesley, "O For a Thousand Tongues to Sing," *The United Methodist Hymnal* (Nashville: The United Methodist Publishing House, 1989), 57.

convict. Compelled to admit the truth

condemn. London. Reprehensible. To criticize. To voice disapproval of

CHAPTER 7

LOVE THAT WILL NOT LET ME GO

For I am convinced that [nothing] will be able to separate us from the love of God in Christ Jesus our Lord.

(Romans 8:38-39)

Adults sometimes have a smiling put-down for those who are younger, especially those in a certain period of their teens. "She's not in love with anybody in particular," we say. "She's just in love with love." Of course that condition isn't necessarily limited to young people, and it's not really all bad. Nearly all of us are in love with love, and it's right and natural that this is so. A rollicking little song insists that it's love that makes the world go round. It is, indeed, because all of us want to love and to be loved. No wonder then that we not only love persons, we love the very idea of love itself.

I was a pastor for nearly forty years, so I have been blessed with an unusual opportunity to observe love and to observe it in a wide range of human life. I doubt that there is any other occupation that provides such variety. A minister performs weddings, thus participating in the primary ritual of love. A minister is likely also to be at the hospital for the birth of a baby, an event that opens floodgates of new expressions for love. And then there are baptisms, confirmations, graduation exercises, and special community events where honors—loving honors!—are conferred and where families want their pastor to be present to celebrate the happiness with them. And of course there are those other human experiences where a clergy person is almost surely present: the hospital vigil, sometimes at the very end of life, the circle of love at a funeral or a memorial service, the solemn walk to the graveside. If anyone has opportunities to see the beauty, the strength, the trials, and the grandeur of human love, surely it is a minister.

But you may already be ahead of me in thinking of those occasions when a minister is compelled also to observe the boundaries and limits of human love. A minister performs weddings but also counsels at times of divorce. We rejoice in the wonder of friendship, especially as we see it develop and grow in church groups. But we also see the transitoriness and mobility of life, which means that many fine friendships at last settle into a note on a Christmas card. And sometimes—Lord, have mercy—we weep with someone who has seen a friendship broken by betrayal or by the mundane commonness of neglect. I ponder now and again the wisdom of a wall-hanging in a Frankfort, Kentucky, bookstore: "What I know about love is what a three-legged dog knows about automobiles." Human love can be beautiful beyond expression, but it can also be achingly sad.

We want so much to be secure in love. We want to know that love can be counted on. But inevitably human love has to let us go—and in some instances, worse than that, it lets us down. Some years ago a careful medical study demonstrated statistically that human relationships are a significant factor in human longevity. Thus, persons in loving relationships of family and marriage live longer. But the catch-22 is this: when we fall in love, marry, have children, or establish family bonds or deep friendships we take a calculated risk that death or some other factor will break the relationship, leaving us more destitute than ever. The study's author concluded that it is better to have loved and lost than never to have loved at all, but he also acknowledged that love is a perilous venture because our human relationships are always susceptible to one kind or another of rupture or intrusion.

When Sheldon and Davy Vanauken fell in love, they believed they had found the perfect relationship, and they intended to keep it that way. They raised what they called "The Shining Barrier," "a fortified place with the walls and watchtowers gleaming white ... protecting the green trees of our love."[1] As one reads their story one has a feeling that Sheldon and Davy came as close as human beings can to maintaining an inviolate love. Yet one day, when they were still in their thirties and when life was so beautiful, Davy died, and their love suffered death's violent physical separation.

Their friend, C. S. Lewis—Sheldon's intellectual mentor and in time their unique companion in Christ—wrote in a way that Vanauken called "severe and splendid." "I sometimes wonder whether bereavement is not, at bottom, the easiest and least perilous of the ways in which men lose the happiness of youthful love. For I believe it must *always* be lost in some way: every merely natural love has to be crucified before it can achieve resurrection."[2] It is the nature of human love to fail—sometimes because we human beings fail, through selfishness or lapse of feeling, and sometimes because natural circumstances, including death, intrude upon our relationships, sometimes even destroying the relationships. Mind you, death doesn't destroy true human love, but obviously it brings a limit or a boundary to it.

So see our human predicament. We need love so much—and we need it partly because of the security it brings. But we know human love must in some way "fail" us, simply because it is human, and thus is victimized by time and space and circumstances altogether beyond our control—to say nothing of the problems that come through our simple human failures. And love comes with such a price: namely, that because we love, we are all the more vulnerable to loss. Thus, some tough-minded people argue that it is better not to have loved, because when you love and lose, your loss makes you more a victim of loneliness or regret than if you had never loved.

Clearly, then, we need the kind of love described by the title of this chapter, a love that will not let us go, a love that will never fail or disappear or be affected by the vagaries of normal human existence.

I have taken my title from a famous hymn-poem written more than a century ago by George Matheson, a minister in the Scottish Free Church.

> O Love that wilt not let me go,
>   I rest my weary soul in thee;
> I give thee back the life I owe,
>   that in thine ocean depths its flow
>   may richer, fuller be.[3]

Matheson said that he composed the hymn on June 6, 1882, in the manse of Innellan, the small parish on the Firth of Clyde where he was then the minister. It was the day of his sister's marriage, and he was alone. "Something had happened to me which was known only to myself, and which caused me the most severe mental suffering. The hymn was the fruit of that suffering."

Albert Edward Bailey, the noted twentieth-century student of Christianity and the arts, tried to put together the pieces to interpret Matheson's veiled words. During Matheson's adolescence he fell deeply in love with a girl, and it appeared the feeling was mutual. But it was discovered that he was going blind, and when the girl learned this, she broke the relationship. At eighteen, he was totally blind. He never married; perhaps because he never fell in love again or perhaps because he was sure no one would want to marry him. Now, more than twenty years after his own deep emotional disappointment, on the day when his sister was being married—thus reminding him of the heartbreak of his own life—alone at home, he wrote. "I had the impression," Matheson said, "rather of having it dictated to me by some inward voice than of working it out myself."[4] I think it is fair to say that George Matheson had learned that human love can let us go. Sometimes a rational element asserts itself in our human love, and we act accordingly. It surely could have seemed to the poet-preacher that human love had abandoned him at just the time he needed most desperately to have its strength and compassion. But another love had sustained him, a love that would not let him go, no matter what his circumstances.

This is the quality of love the Apostle Paul celebrates in the closing phrases of the eighth chapter of his Letter to the Romans. "Who shall separate us from the love of Christ?" The apostle centers the issue with his rhetorical question, then raises the stakes higher and higher as he adds a series of questions—and then moves into a series of affirmations:

> Who will separate us from the love of Christ? Will hardship, or distress, or persecution, or famine, or nakedness, or peril, or sword? . . . No, in all these things we are more than conquerors through him who loved us. For I am convinced that neither death, nor life, nor angels, nor rulers, nor things present, nor things to come, nor powers, nor height, nor depth, nor anything else in all creation, will be able to separate us from the love of God in Christ Jesus our Lord. (Romans 8:35, 37-39)

But see what a realist Paul is? He doesn't close his eyes—nor will he let us close ours—to the facts of the world in which we live. He reminds us, forcefully, that in our living and our dying we will encounter every imaginable kind of struggle and test. Paul feels it so deeply that his accounting isn't carefully organized. The apostle dictated his letters, and this passage is one of those instances where we readers get the feeling that he is dictating while in a rising tide of excitement so that the words come in a cascade of emotion.

But he covers the gamut of possible conflict and struggle. He begins with the rhetorical questions: shall tribulation, distress, persecution, famine, nakedness, peril, or sword separate us from the love of Christ? Paul was drawing his list from his own biography; he knew all of these issues at first hand. If a lesser soul were writing we might discount his or her list as an exercise in bravado. But not Paul! He had been beaten, stoned, and imprisoned for his faith and had known many kinds of peril. When he asks if any of these can separate us from the love of Christ, I'm satisfied to let him answer his own question. "You know better than I do, Paul! You've traveled the road you describe. You've put this love to the test. You speak from experience."

I am sure that I am writing to some persons who can underline large portions of Paul's statement from their own experiences. You have, yourself, gone through distress and peril and physical and emotional pain and have found that none of these have separated you from the love of Christ. Indeed, they have only made that love more real.

But Paul isn't done. Now he asks some of the questions that he senses might be in the minds of his readers. He imagines someone saying, "But death will separate us from the love of Christ"—perhaps reflecting some of the very questions we've raised from our experiences with human love—and Paul answers, "No, no; it can't, because he is eternal, so his love overarches death." Then Paul anticipates the question: "But life can separate—just the very daily-ness of it, the humdrum that wears one down and reduces all emotions to ordinariness"—and Paul answers, "No, nothing in life can break the love of Christ."

At this point the apostle takes us beyond the ordinary language of our human existence into the realm of the spiritual world. He speaks of angels, principalities, powers—mysteries of life that are quite beyond easy definition, and because they are beyond such easy definition they are often pushed aside by some as superstition or as primitive concepts that we have now outgrown. But if we are honest and realistic, we know better: we know that Paul is speaking the truth. Who has not said at some point, "I'm so discouraged, so frightened, so depressed," and have been the more troubled because we can't find obvious reason for our feelings. Paul may seem to some more of a poet than a scientist when he writes of "principalities and powers," but he is also an altogether honest realist. If you have wrestled with the demons of despair or self-hatred or irrational loneliness, you know that these powers may be hard to put into scientific terms, but they are real, no doubt of that. And at such a point it is magnificent to know that *none* of these things can separate us from the love of Christ.

But still, Paul is not done. What he knows of the love of Christ is of such dimensions that he wants to be sure not only that he has covered all he has experienced thus far in his long and perilous journey but also that he has anticipated what any of his followers might have known. So he goes into the facts of the present and the possibilities of the future. Can either of these separate us from the love of Christ? Definitely not! The present is within God's control, and the future is more surely God's than ours. Then Paul introduces two words that seem simple enough in English but carry a good deal more meaning in the New Testament Greek in which Paul was writing and which was the daily language of his readers in Corinth.

Neither height nor depth, Paul said, can separate us from the love of Christ. In the Greek of Paul's day, these two words were astrological terms, height referring to the time when a star was at its zenith and depth when it was at its lowest. A good many people in that first-century world—like ours, I regret to say—watched their astrological charts. Some of them said, "The stars are against me; I'm doomed at this time, under this sign." Paul set the matter right: neither height nor depth can separate us from the love of Christ.

Paul sums up the matter in one encompassing term, as if to take care of any other possibilities his readers might raise. He was convinced, he said, that not anything "in all creation" was able to bring about such a separation. Paul throws out a gauntlet—to doubter, to troubled soul, to cynic, yes, to hell itself: You name it: there is nothing that can interfere with this love.

Why was Paul so sure? Was this Paul the philosopher-theologian, matching thoughts with the kind of people he had met on Mars Hill? Was this declaration a product of his training under Gamaliel and his years of matching intellectual swords with fellow rabbis?

Well, I'm sure Paul's philosophical training and his Jewish heritage buttressed and refined what he had to say. But in the end, Paul was speaking not as a theorist but as a practitioner. He knew what it was to be disappointed in people, and to have good and earnest people fall short of his expectations. He was living daily with some incurable affliction; he never tells us what. He belonged to the smallest minority movement in the first-century world. Sometimes his prayers seemed futile. But in it all he knew something, knew it beyond argument—the love of God that had been manifested in his life through Jesus Christ. That love had reached Paul at the time he was striving so passionately to destroy it. Such love, Paul knew by experience, was indestructible. It would never let him—or anyone—go.

Some nineteen centuries after Paul lived, a great Scottish preacher, Arthur John Gossip, returned to his pulpit for the first time after the dramatically sudden and unexpected death of his beloved wife. He shared in sensitive, shaded fashion where his faith stood at the time and concluded with a reference to Bunyan's *Pilgrim's Progress*: "I too, like Hopeful, can call back to you who one day in your turn will have to cross [the Jordan], 'Be of good cheer, my friend, for I feel the bottom, and it is sound.'"[5]

Sound, indeed! It is a love that will not, can not, let us go, because its foundation is in our Lord Christ. Nothing can break it, nothing. The secret is in him, in Christ.

NOTES

1. Sheldon Vanauken, *A Severe Mercy* (San Francisco: Harper & Row, 1977), 36.

2. Ibid., 211.

3. George Matheson, "O Love That Wilt Not Let Me Go," *The United Methodist Hymnal* (Nashville: The United Methodist Publishing House, 1989), 480.

4. Albert Edward Bailey, *The Gospel in Hymns* (New York: Charles Scribner's Sons, 1950), 457-60.

5. A. J. Gossip, "But When Life Tumbles In, What Then?" *20 Centuries of Great Preaching* (Waco, TX: Word Books, 1971), Volume 8, 239.

CHAPTER 8

ON BEING A FINISHED PRODUCT

And I am sure that he who began a good work in you will bring it to completion at the day of Jesus Christ.

(Philippians 1:6 RSV)

I met George Beverly Shea a great many years ago, before his role as Billy Graham's featured soloist made his voice and face famous around the world. Shea already was established, however, as a radio personality through his daily broadcast for Club Aluminum, and I was seeking his services to do a free broadcast for a world relief agency. He accepted my request without hesitation and gave a valuable Saturday morning to a cause to which he had no tie other than his readiness to serve Christ wherever he could.

Many years later a religious publication asked several popular Christian personalities to name their favorite Bible verse. George Beverly Shea quoted Philippians 1:6: "And I am sure that he who began a good work in you will bring it to completion at the day of Jesus Christ."

I can't profess to know Mr. Shea well enough to make a truly significant observation, but let me simply say that I wasn't surprised to learn that this was his key verse. It is consistent with what I have observed and learned about his extended years of Christian commitment. His witness to the verse is far better than mine, but I look to this verse, too, as one of the promises of Scripture that have nourished my soul and spirit over the years.

I believe there is something in every human being that hungers to become a "finished product." We humans are born with the instinct, so to speak, to grow. At first this growth is an involuntary matter, and nature itself takes care of most of the details. Our bodies grow as rapidly as we provide the nourishment they seek. Our minds, too, grow at the rate at which they're fed. Unfortunately, we don't hear the mind when it cries for nourishment—the mind's cry is not as audible as the stomach's—so in too many instances the infant mind is not fed as faithfully as the infant body.

And then there is another area of growth, one more subtle in its demands and thus more easily overlooked; but ironically, it is an area more crucial than our mental development and ultimately more of an issue than even our physical existence. I'm speaking of those matters having to do with our character and our spirit. We humans are born with the same insistent hunger for spiritual growth as for food for our bodies; we long instinctively to be better than we are. Our bodies, by their nature, insist on growing up. Our souls have the same insistence, but they rarely get the same attention. This biblical promise assures us that it is God's will for us to grow up spiritually and that God intends to bring this process "to completion."

The promise comes to us in a little New Testament book, Saint Paul's Letter to the people at Philippi. This book is often spoken of as "the Epistle of Joy" because of the mood that pervades its several pages. The apostle was writing from prison—the price he was once again paying for preaching the gospel—but his pride and pleasure in the congregation at Philippi seemed to make his imprisonment of no significance. Paul had great expectations for his people at Philippi. He believed they were en route to perfection, and he told them so. As he writes, I imagine him picturing the little congregation: shopkeepers, slaves, a few artisans, most of them unlearned and common. On the surface they didn't appear to be much. But Paul was utterly, serenely confident that each one would someday be a finished product.

I think Paul's feelings might be compared with those of a dedicated kindergarten or first-grade teacher. She looks out on her new class on the opening school day in September. Some of them are a little more scrubbed and groomed than they will be later in the year, when the newness of the semester has worn off, but even at best they are a mixed lot. Probably not one can read (that's why they've come to school!) nor can many, if any, form good letters. Yet looking at these five-year-olds the teacher can imagine that one of them will someday be a neurosurgeon, another a respected businesswoman, still another a community leader, and perhaps one will be a teacher, like herself. She sees a potential, a magnificent potential, if only they will grow in knowledge and dedication.

But even as I write I realize that my illustration is poor. Paul is anticipating so much more. If the kindergarten teacher is realistic, she will confess to herself later that only one or two of this class, at best, will reach the kind of heights she envisions; the majority will settle for very modest achievements and some will perhaps slip off into indifference and failure. Saint Paul, however, was entertaining his high expectations not for a select few with superior potential, but for the whole, mixed, in-and-out group. His promise is to all of them: "Of this I am confident, that he who has begun the good work in you will go on completing it until the day of Jesus Christ" (Philippians 1:6 Moffatt).

And more. Intellectual or vocational achievement is relatively simple to attain compared to achievement in character and soul. We can tell the prospective student some rules which, if obeyed, will almost surely mean success. But growth in spirit is so much more complex and the problems and pitfalls so much more numerous and subtle.

I am encouraged by what Paul writes. I want so much, myself, to be a finished product someday! When I look at myself I see so many rough edges, so many elements that are crude and disappointing. In truth, after all these years I still see areas of my life where it looks as if I haven't even begun. Since childhood, I have numbered among my favorite hymns what was probably originally an old prayer meeting song:

> I'm pressing on the upward way,
> New heights I'm gaining every day;
> Still praying as I'm onward bound,
> "Lord, plant my feet on higher ground."[1]

Some days I feel I'm making progress toward that higher ground, but then again the gains seem questionable. But the apostle won't let me settle into defeat or spiritual mediocrity. "I am convinced," he says to my soul, "that someday you will be a finished product!"

And what I covet for myself, I covet for you. More likely than not, I've never met you. But I'm your fellow pilgrim, and I'm on your side. I want you to achieve. If I knew you, I would want you to enjoy health and worthy success in your work and fulfillment in your relationships. But I have a still higher goal for you and for me. I want us to attain the qualities of character and of true, profound goodness that symbolize Christian life at its best. I want us to become finished products!

Now, of course, it's altogether possible that you aren't enthusiastic about my dreams for you. When I say that I want you to become a finished product, there's a hint that I don't think you're just fine the way you are now. Perhaps you'd like to straighten out my thinking—in which case I'm glad I'm not in easy reach at this moment. It's just that I see so much more potential in both you and me than some folks see. It's so easy, you know, to settle for the lowlands of life and to write off our potential by looking at some shortcoming and saying, "Well, you'll have to take it or leave it, because that's just the way I am." Why cooperate with the lower level when you are innately equipped to reach higher?

The Greek philosopher Socrates memorably said, "The unexamined life is not worth living." Christianity pushes us further. The gospel insists that the ungrowing life is not worth living. We ought indeed to examine our lives to see where we fall short and to anticipate our potential, but examination isn't enough (as I'm sure Socrates would agree). After seeing where we are, we need to correct, improve, and grow. Heaven made us to be growing creatures, and if we abdicate that calling, we miss the very purpose of our being. And if there is any meaning in the biblical term, "born again," it is to tell us that the purpose of our encountering God and grace is that we shall grow up. We are born not to be perpetual infants but to reach holy maturity.

But sometimes this business of growing up becomes quite discouraging. Do you remember the myth of Sisyphus? He was condemned to roll a huge stone to the top of a high hill, but each time he reached the top, the stone rolled back down. Some of our efforts at spiritual maturity seem to follow just such a pattern. We struggle to be more disciplined in the devotional life, more kindly in the things we say, more considerate of other people, and for a time it looks as if we're succeeding. Then, suddenly and sadly, our efforts come tumbling down life's hill. I spoke earlier of the kindergarten teacher who looks out on her five-year-old charges on the opening day of a school term and envisions their best potential. It occurs to me that it is easier to see the potential of five-year-olds on the first day than it is to continue believing in the potential of eighth-graders in the middle of February. Just as it is in our own lives! We have high hopes for ourselves on the day of conversion or of rededication or during a high moment of new resolve, but it's more difficult to be hopeful about ourselves in the low and routine places of life. Nothing is so hard on the sense of achievement as the ordinariness of life—and life is made up primarily of ordinary days.

The Apostle Paul put the matter in spiritual terms for his congregants at Philippi. His terms need some explaining for us, however, because they come from a different language and a different culture. The Philippians lived in the midst of a pagan world where their neighbors made sacrifices to their gods. The ritual began with a ceremony that was known by the technical term *enarchesthai,* which is the word Paul uses when he says that God has *begun* a good work in us. When the whole ritual was complete, the Greeks used the word *epitelein.* This is the word Paul uses when he says that God will *complete* the work.[2] The apostle, that is, was dramatizing to the people that they were themselves a spiritual sacrifice in which God was at work. If we are *God's* spiritual project, the idea of our someday becoming a "finished product" is much more hopeful.

But it's right that we should be plagued by the question about our prospects. How can we hope, really, to become a finished product? If you and I have a grand vision of the kind of person we'd like to be, aren't we committing ourselves to a mission of futility? Something like 175 years ago a pioneer Methodist preacher in North Carolina, Melville B. Cox, wrote in his journal, "I want a *holy* heart. And He who has begotten the struggle for it, I trust, will grant it unto me." I think Cox summed up the matter rightly—indeed, that he was affirming what the apostle had in mind. This hunger for completeness that you and I have is not something we came up with on our own. It isn't a product of our unaided imagination. Thus, Saint Paul was confident that the one who first set the hunger in our souls, the one who gave us the restless longing for perfection, is the one who will work with us to the point of our completion. The one who planted the impulse in us will work with us for its fulfillment.

I hope you feel as reassured by this as I do. God is not given to unfinished business. God doesn't do halfway jobs.

So consider: God has begun a good work in you, and he wants to complete it. This is the divine intention. I mentioned earlier that this verse is the favorite of George Beverly Shea. In explaining why, Mr. Shea said, "Many years ago, I began to feel the presence of Christ in the formative years. I didn't know what I was preparing for. . . ." We never really do know, do we? Who can say when he or she sets out on the Christian life what the years ahead may hold, what prospects routine and wonderful, may lie ahead? For Mr. Shea, the passage of time has brought dramatic opportunities for service in almost every part of the world, activities that have made him a public personality. He sums up the matter, "I have confidence that God will remain with me until my work is finished."[3] I think one might add, "Until God's work in me is finished."

I am encouraged, too, by the patience of God. God has the time necessary to wait me out. How wonderful, since I am sometimes slow, sometimes dull, sometimes even rebellious. Occasionally I read on the sports page that a particular athlete is being released because the team can't afford the time that will be necessary for this player to "develop"—that is, to fulfill what they had anticipated was his or her potential. I am grateful that God has the time to wait me out (and you too!), and is *willing* to wait us out. Here is grace, extended. Some of us progress slowly and erratically; human advisors might give up on us. But God has the time and the patience to see us through.

Michelangelo—whose genius ranged through sculpture, painting, architecture, and poetry—is often described as a person who was torn between the ache for perfection and the despair of failure. But he was sustained by the knowledge that God was with him in his work. In 1528, he put these feelings into a sonnet. He spoke of the "rude hammer" with which he brought shape out of the stones in his sculpting, and he confessed that he was dependent upon the "divine hammer" that was at work in his own life. He concluded:

So my unfinished work will fall short
If now the divine workshop does not give me
That help to make it which is alone in this world.[4]

Our lives have such grand potential for goodness and character. But they are like the great, cragged rocks on which the sculptor works—crude objects, with the glory locked inside and quite invisible unless some artist dreams of a potential that no one else can see, and in which he or she will then invest the fine, sometimes harsh work of hammer and chisel.

God is this ultimate artist. But we should remember that God leaves a major share of the divine artistry in the hands of various subcontractors. Some are skilled and helpful, but some are crude to the point of peril. To be honest, I doubt that God has employed some of these subcontractors; I think they get involved in sacred projects simply because they think they can help or perhaps even because they simply enjoy meddling. And I marvel at this, that God so often uses even the most inept intruders as collaborators in the process of bringing shape and beauty into our lives. I can think of several people who came at me with rough and untrained hammers but for whom I now give thanks to God. It is not for their skills that I am grateful but for their intentions and for the way God folded those intentions into other elements in bringing some surprising beauty into my life. I sometimes think I have benefited as much from unskilled laborers as from the artists of faith and learning who have come my way. This, too, is a marvel of grace, and for it I am unceasingly grateful.

As the process moves along I have come more and more to feel that I am not so concerned about the process itself as long as I see the prospect of the finished product. I marvel at the grace of God that, in the familiar language of John Newton, "saved a wretch like me." But I marvel still more at the grace that continues to manifest itself in divine patience as God watches patiently my slow growth in spirit and character, and keeps believing in my potential.

Especially, I encourage myself by the promise the Apostle Paul made to the people at Philippi and which I believe God's Spirit extends as well to you and me: "He who began a good work in you will bring it to completion at the day of Jesus Christ." I expect some day to be a finished product. God is willing if I am. And so, too, for you. This is a promise to keep us, and to spur us on.

I choose Him

NOTES

1. Johnson Oatman, Jr., "Higher Ground," *Favorite Hymns of Praise* (Chicago: Tabernacle Publishing Company, 1972), 262.
2. William Barclay, *The Letters to the Philippians, Colossians, and Thessalonians* (Philadelphia: The Westminster Press, 1959), 19-20.
3. *Christian Life*, February, 1978, page 31.
4. Frederick Hartt, *Michaelangelo: The Complete Sculpture* (New York: H. N. Abrams, 1980), 13.

CHAPTER 9

RESOURCE UNLIMITED

I can do all things through him who strengthens me.
(Philippians 4:13)
My God shall supply all your need according to his riches in glory by Christ Jesus. (Philippians 4:19 KJV)

My biggest problem when I set out to write this book was to limit the number of promises I would discuss with you. At one point I thought of doing a survey, perhaps of my students or of a church where I worship or even of some of my readers, to make this a book of favorite biblical promises as revealed through the experiences of others. This didn't seem quite right, however, because I knew this book ought to be a personal witness. But to hold myself to a dozen or even a baker's dozen was quite frustrating. The faithfulness of God in my life can't be fenced in by such modest boundaries.

But I knew that some verses simply couldn't be left out. Such is the case with the direction I'm heading just now. It may seem to you that I'm cheating just a bit, since I'm using two verses. But they belong to the same general passage in Paul's Letter to the Philippians, and they're dealing with the same general principle of life. "I can do all things through him who strengthens me," and "My God shall supply all your need according to his riches in glory by Christ Jesus."

Both verses are testimonies from the apostle—in the first instance a direct declaration of Paul's own abounding courage, and in the other an exhortation to his readers, encouraging them to know that their way is secure in Jesus Christ.

I have to confess, however, that in some sense these verses had a greater existential meaning to me many years ago than they do today. This realization makes me more than a little uneasy. I suppose I have the feeling expressed by those who are either cynical enough or superstitious enough to say, "Aren't you testing fate," but if I am it is in the pursuit of honesty. I don't want to witness to you in language beyond my spiritual state.

Here's what I mean. As I have indicated at other times in my writing and speaking, I grew up that period of American history known as the Great Depression. The Depression reached our family when I was in the fifth grade, and it was still a dominant issue when I graduated from high school. And because I was the only child left at home during most of those years, our finances were never a mystery to me. Sometimes I was an accomplice, so to speak, in deflecting trouble. When my parents didn't have a full month's rent at hand, they sent me with a temporary half-payment, knowing the landlord wouldn't express his unhappiness or his threats to a boy. I would become quite tedious if I would illustrate further, and I suspect my stories would sound like those proverbial tales of winter weather reported by your grandparents, who "walked to school and back through snow, uphill both ways."

We survived it all remarkably well. There were many secrets to our survival—one of them being that a good percentage of our friends were in the same state and another being that we were so confident of the promises of God. A rhythm plays in the back of my mind and soul. As my parents visited with their church friends, someone almost surely would confess that their finances were now at the last penny—literally. And someone almost surely would answer, "Don't forget the promise: 'My God shall supply all your needs according to his riches in glory by Christ Jesus.'" In so many such instances the situation was honestly quite hopeless. Yet somehow, against all odds, these great souls refused to be taken captive by hopelessness. I wonder how often, in those frightful days, I saw the "hopeless" soul of a few days before standing up in a midweek prayer meeting to tell how God had seen him or her through still another crisis.

So here's the point of the matter just now: I don't hear those verses quoted as frequently as I once did. I suppose I could interrupt myself to say that we don't hear as much quoting of any kind as we used to hear. I won't try to explain it, but I ponder often that the people of my parent's generation had a storehouse of favorite sayings—a major share from the Bible, but a substantial number from other sources known and unidentified.

But especially I don't come upon many people who live by the philosophy of the two promises we're discussing just now. In the early seventeenth century somebody said, "Man's extremity is God's opportunity." People quote such a word only when they find themselves at a place of human extremity, and the verses before us are verses meant for extreme times. But we have fewer experiences with life's extremities because a larger share of life seems now to be within the measure of human possibility.

Of course, what I'm now saying reflects life as we know it in middle-class and upper-middle-class America. We would get a different report from Christians in Africa and the slums and remote villages of South America. Such persons still live with a constant sense of their need of God's help; they need miracles almost daily. But in truth so, too, do some millions of Americans. I remember the late Dr. George Buttrick reminiscing on the congregation he served in New York City. It was divided roughly between Fifth Avenue and Park Avenue wealth on the one hand and tenement poverty on the other. "Every day is a crisis in the tenements," Dr. Buttrick said. I'm very sure that if you or I were to go to several million homes in America's ghettoes, both urban and rural, we would find that for those who know the Scriptures, one of the most beloved scripture promises is still, "My God shall supply all your needs...."

Am I saying that these verses are no longer significant for many of us, or that their significance is limited to a few crucial life experiences? By no means! If that were so I wouldn't bother to include this chapter in this book. In a sense, our need for these verses increases as our way of life becomes more successful and complicated. Unfortunately, we aren't as likely to look to God for help, because we've become accustomed to relying on the many resources that our wealth or connections or knowledge make available to us. Let me put it this way: when as a teenager I was asked to preach in some little church, my resources were my personal library of perhaps a dozen books, my Bible, prayer, and disciplined thinking. Now I sit surrounded by hundreds of books (for which I am profoundly thankful). It is easy for me to turn to those books too soon, not relying enough on disciplined thinking and the resources of prayer. And for those who are computer-competent, I suspect that the internet has pushed not only books to the background but also God-dependence and the use of one's own creative gifts.

We never grow beyond our need to draw upon the resources of God. I am certain that the reason George Washington Carver never lost his genius for discovery is because as a world-heralded scientist he still clung to the faith of the barefoot slave boy who had a way with plants. He bowed daily before God as he pursued widening frontiers of discovery. By sorry contrast I think of Israel's first king, Saul. Early in his reign he was humble before both God and his people. But the privilege of power was more than he could handle. Before long he was assuming rights that were not his to claim and seeking adulation that eventually became a deadly intoxication. The greater his kingdom and the greater his successes, the more Saul needed God. Unfortunately, he didn't see it that way until it was too late and until his life and throne were caught in a deadly downward spiral.

Oliver Cromwell is remembered as a man of iron will. A born military genius, he never knew what it was to lose on the battlefield. But at the death of his son, Cromwell was plunged into darkness. He said that the verse, "I can do all things through Christ who strengthenths me" was "one beam in a dark place."[1] Quite surely, it saved his life. It is fortunate that with all the strength of his personality and of his position, Cromwell never forgot how to draw upon the resource he had found in God.

Cromwell's experience also reminds us that our lives are made up of so many quite different parts. We can be rich in one area and poverty-stricken in another. Some who have property are short on friends—and just as surely, some who have friends in abundance may be destitute in property. I've known some who were wealthy in reputation yet—ironically—sadly lacking in self-respect; one got the feeling they had worked overtime at building themselves up to others in order to make up for the lack they felt within. And of course there are so many persons who are wealthy in business or politics or the arts who know themselves to be failures as parents.

Which is to say, there aren't many who do not at one time or another know what it is to be in need. Wealth has innumerable measuring sticks, and to be rich in one by no means guarantees abundance in others. And while Paul's primary emphasis in this promise was material needs, he wouldn't have limited himself to that area of life. When he said, "My God shall supply *all* your need" I believe he intended to embrace the whole vast realm of human need: material, intellectual, social, spiritual—you name it.

All of which leads us to the phrase that is the key in both of these promises. "I can do all things," Paul said; but how? *Through [Christ] who strengthens me.*" "My God shall supply all your need," Paul promised the people at Philippi. And again, but how? "According to his riches in glory *by Christ Jesus*." If one is going to employ an utterly inclusive word like *all*, one had better have an utterly inclusive resource on which to draw. This was Paul's secret, the secret he was sharing so vigorously and unreservedly with the Philippians—and through them, with us. Paul's secret was Jesus Christ.

This was no idle statement on Paul's part. He had told the Philippians earlier in his letter that he had once been a very well-to-do person, and he listed his advantages by way of a brief biographical sketch. He had a grand family heritage, impeccable ethnic roots, religious upbringing—and then he had added to it his own personal righteousness ("self-righteousness," some would have said) and his membership in the exclusive body of the Pharisees. But he looked upon all of this as "a loss" once he came to see "the surpassing value of knowing Christ Jesus my Lord. For his sake I have suffered the loss of all things, and I regard them as rubbish, in order that I may gain Christ and be found in him" (Philippians 3:8-9).

Jesus spoke in one of his parables of a merchant who was in search of fine pearls. One day when he found one "of great value, he went and sold all that he had and bought it" (Matthew 13:46). Paul could justifiably have pointed to himself as a fulfillment of Jesus' story. He "sold everything" to get Christ, and in doing so he knew beyond doubt that he had gotten an eternal bargain. Because now, as Paul understood it, there were no boundaries on his life. He could do all things through Christ, and with this same Christ there was no need that could not be met.

This brings me round to the title by which I have encompassed the two promises we are discussing: *Resource Unlimited*. I am speaking not of *resources*, as in money, education, talents, or human favor, all of which obviously are very attractive; I am speaking of the ultimate Resource, Jesus Christ.

When you analyze it this way, you realize that Paul was not really irrational when he sold everything to get his pearl of great price. Our other resources are all so fragile, even on this earth, to say nothing of eternity. We learned in the first decade of this twenty-first century that even the fabled names of finance can collapse and fortunes can be swept away. I have great regard for talent, but talent can slip from us as easily as the arm of a baseball pitcher, the timbre of an entertainer's voice, the sure touch of a surgeon's hand. I think often of a magnificent athlete who was later elected into the National Football League Hall of Fame. I once heard him say, "Every time I pull on my uniform, I know that if one wrong twist catches my knee, my career is ended." He had a precise measure for judging his career security. Not many can speak so specifically, but all of us walk on such a razor's edge of insecurity.

So Paul was radical, but he was not foolish. *Radical,* you may remember, comes from the Latin word for root (as in *radish*). To be truly radical, one goes to the root of a matter. And when Paul declared that he had given up everything in order to get Christ, he was declaring himself to be radical: he had gotten to the root of life's issues. All else might pass away—all systems, governments, plans, and persons might fail. But then, still and always, there was Christ.

I said earlier that we don't quote these two verses as often and as earnestly as some of us used to and indeed as the generation before mine did. This is unfortunate because these two promises are as true as ever and as appropriate to our lives as ever. The nature of our need may change from time to time and in some ways from generation to generation, and our definition of life's extremities may also change. But the *resource* is as adequate for the executive as for the alcoholic (or indeed, for the executive who is an alcoholic), and it is as important to a middle-aged achiever as to a youthful beginner. Or, to turn the generations and the situations around, these verses are as important to the young person who is full of expectation as to the middle-aged who has come to accept defeat as an inevitable in life's journey.

Some of the issues you and I bring to the light of these promises are obvious. Some wonder how they will get one more child through college and others how long they will have to work beyond the time they'd originally planned to retire—and to wonder, also, whether they'll be able to get and keep a job for that long. And some, inevitably, are facing the challenge of major surgery, while others grope for strength to rebuild after the death of someone dearly loved.

But other needs are not so easily seen. Because I was a pastor for so long, and probably also because I simply have an innate sympathy for our human race, I have been made sad by the secret sadnesses that people carry and that surface now and then in pensive moments of real conversation. I'm thinking, for instance, of those persons who live far below their potential because they've never realized the great potential they've carried. I don't mean that every person should be Shakespeare or Milton or Rachmaninov; I mean simply that there is beauty and capacity in so many people that is beyond their imagining but that somehow, nevertheless, makes them restless and just a little sad. I'm thinking, too, of someone who is troubled by middle-aged ennui: you've gotten so much, but the flavor just isn't there, whether in work or family or marriage or fun. And I'm thinking also of someone who would never admit it, but who desperately dreads growing old, losing physical attractiveness, or watching some of his or her most admired skills slipping away.

Whatever the situation, I offer a tandem promise, as the apostle offered it nearly twenty centuries ago to the Christians at Philippi. And although I haven't won all of the battles that have come my way and although I can't claim to have held fast to these two promises in every circumstance, I've lived with them long enough, in a wide enough variety of times and places, to know beyond doubt that they are true. Listen:

"I can do all things through [Christ] who strengthens me."

"My God shall supply all your need according to his riches in glory by Christ Jesus."

This is the Resource Unlimited. In a world where the negatives seem sometimes so dominant and where the positives seem too often to fail, I recommend Paul's wisdom. There is a Resource, Jesus Christ, and there is no boundary that fences him in, neither in power to perform nor in willingness to meet our needs.

Take my word for it. Or better yet, take Paul's. This is a promise that will keep you.

NOTE

1. Thomas Carlyle, *Oliver Cromwell's Letters and Speeches: With Elucidations* (London: Chapman and Hall, 1899), 80.

CHAPTER 10

DON'T GIVE UP!

*So let us not grow weary in doing what is right, for we will
reap at harvest time, if we do not give up.* (Galatians 6:9)

I confess to being an optimist and, more than that, I'm
glad of it. I have sometimes invested my optimism in poor
causes and probably sometimes in unlikely people. My optimism would sometimes have been better if it had been
tempered by more research or better judgment. Over the
years some of my optimism has been corrected by experience. But when all the accounts are settled, I am grateful
for being an optimist, and if I had my life to live over I
would ask not only for my current quota of optimism but
even for a dose more.

It seems clear that our ancestors deserve much of the
credit and at least some of the blame for our temperaments.
I come from a pretty good breed of optimists on both the
Kalas and Barth sides of my family, and for that I am grateful. But whatever can be said for my genes, my attitude toward life is ultimately and primarily the faith in which I was
raised (something for which, again, I can thank my ancestors) and which I have taken for my own. I am a product of
the Holy Scriptures: I have read these scriptures devotion-
ally and thoughtfully for many decades, have heard them
preached and taught, and have sung them in the best of the

hymnody of the church; and those Scriptures, if given even half a chance, will make one an indefatigable optimist.

But not a naïve or superficial one. Biblical optimism is altogether as good with the wind in its face as with the wind at its back. In fact, a large share of the Bible's optimism comes from negative settings in which its stories and its convictions appear, circumstances which would justify throwing in the proverbial towel. It seems as if shouting "Trouble!" to a biblical writer is like shouting "Sic 'em" to a dog. The saints of both the Old and New Testaments seemed invigorated by adversity rather than diminished by it.

And no one more so than the great Apostle Paul. He declares this optimism, this never-give-up spirit repeatedly, but never better and never in a more unlikely place than in his letter to the believers in Galatia.

The apostle often had reason to be disappointed in his converts. This shouldn't have surprised him, nor should it surprise us. Most of Paul's converts came from undisciplined Gentile cultures, settings where immorality and marginal conduct were the norm. In most cases they had little training from Paul and his associates before Paul moved on to other settings, so they were wide open to error in conduct and doctrine as they moved from the first glory of conversion to the more routine years of spiritual testing and growth.

And that's what had happened to the believers in Galatia. It is good to remind ourselves before we get farther into the story to see the Apostle Paul as the author of the key doctrinal writings of the New Testament and as perhaps the single most important voice in the shaping of the early Christian church. But for the people in the first century who heard him preach, Paul was not the person who would eventually lay the groundwork of Christian doctrine; he was just one of a number of preachers and teachers who came their way. And as far as many of the early believers were concerned, he was not the most appealing or the most persuasive. Other teachers had better oratorical skills and apparently others were more physically prepossessing. So after Paul had established churches in given settings, some of his followers were easily influenced by preachers who followed—and some of those preachers had agendas of their own.

This was especially true in Galatia, and Paul's Letter to the Galatians shows it. Sometime probably not too long after Paul had established churches in Galatia, some other Christian teachers came to the area. They were probably Jewish Christians who had deep reverence for the Law of Moses, and because of this loyalty to the Law, they believed and taught that these new Gentile converts should obey the basics of the Mosaic Law, beginning with the rite of circumcision.

No one knew the Jewish Law better than Paul; as he himself put it, "as to the law, a Pharisee" (Philippians 3:5)— that is, a prime exemplar of the law. But Paul was convinced beyond all debate that salvation was in the cross of Christ alone. If anyone in history has believed in "amazing grace" it was Paul. So when Paul heard that the people in the Galatian churches were concluding that the cross was not enough and that they must also be circumcised and probably take on other requirements of the Mosaic Law, he responded passionately. "You foolish Galatians!" he wrote. "Who has bewitched you?" (Galatians 3:1).

So as Paul came to the concluding paragraphs of his letter to the people of Galatia he might have been justified if he had sounded like a soul in retreat, a battered warrior who wonders whether his efforts have been in vain. Instead, Paul rises to his full (if slight) height, adjusts his spiritual armor, and insists, "So let us not grow weary in doing what is right, for we will reap at harvest-time, if we do not give up" (Galatians 6:9).

Nor was Paul writing to people who lived in the sunlight of success and favor. Anyone in the first-century world who chose to follow Jesus Christ was immediately identifying himself with a minority group that was looked upon as enemies of the emperor at worst (since the emperor was to be seen as a god, and Christians said there was only one God) or as naïve dreamers (believers in the resurrection) at best. They not only were following a man who had been executed as a common criminal, they were choosing to say that the cross—the method of Jesus' execution—was their glory and the hope of their salvation.

And Paul said, "Don't give up! Don't get tired of doing what is right! You'll reap at harvest time if you just stand fast." Paul was speaking for himself, for the people of Galatia, and for any and every believer in the centuries since, even to today.

Paul had a head start in his belief in not giving up. This spirit was interwoven through all of his Jewish heritage. It was written into the wisdom literature of his ancestors: "For a righteous man falls seven times, / and rises again" (Proverbs 24:16 RSV). When Paul's ancestors in Israel were being defeated by invading armies, the prophet Jeremiah showed his faith in the future by purchasing the deed for land owned by some of his kin. Jeremiah was assured by the Lord God, "Fields shall be bought for money, and deeds shall be signed and sealed and witnessed, in the land of Benjamin, in the places around Jerusalem, and in the cities of Judah...for I will restore their fortunes, says the LORD" (Jeremiah 32:44). Nearly two generations would pass before the promise of God would be fulfilled, but by his purchase Jeremiah was declaring his faith in the future: don't give up! No matter the size of the opposing army, no matter the forecasts of disaster and the voices of naysayers—don't give up.

I suspect that the stories of churches, religious institutions, and individual lives are replete with instances where believers have lost heart. I think often of what happened at one point in the political history of New York City in the nineteenth century. A corrupt political machine had controlled politics for more than a generation, and there seemed no possibility of a change. But a courageous pastor began organizing church members throughout the city, and the grassroots movement was successful; they won the election. Four years later, however, the old political machine took over again. When someone asked the crusading pastor what had happened, he offered a succinct diagnosis: "The good people got tired of being good before the bad people got tired of being bad."

And what is true of organizations and mass movements is of course multiplied by the thousands in our individual lives. How many college students have settled for mediocre grades when the library research became a grind? How many athletes have lost their dreams of making the team when the wind drills seemed endless? Ponder, too, the struggle between good and bad habits. When I see a testimonial on television for a weight loss program, I notice a line in fine print: "Results not typical." Most people give up on the discipline. The apostle has a word for us: we dare not grow weary in our struggle with the easy way, the low self-expectation, the compromising with our own better instincts.

I am grieved when I hear good, earnest people acquiesce to evil. Christians should be the last to give up on politics, especially in a democracy. At the report of still another cause being lost to lobbyists or another leader selling out to special interests, some are quick to say, "They're all the same. They're all crooks." This kind of cynicism may sound tough-minded, but it isn't; it's soft and cowardly and defeatist. Those who sign up for goodness need to remember that the battle will be long and the opposition will be strong, well-financed, and often ruthless. The fight against evil is never easy, whether the battle ground is political, economic, moral, or social—or whether it is simply the private struggle within one's own soul.

That is, the struggle for righteousness and justice is not for the faint of heart. I traveled through much of Africa in September 1961, in countries then known as Kenya,

Nyasaland, Southern Rhodesia, the Republic of South Africa, Nigeria, and Ghana—the names of some have changed in the meanwhile. I remember the enthusiasm of young African leaders in so many of those countries. They saw the end of colonialism and the prospect of a new world of political freedom. Most of them had little knowledge of governance, but they were intoxicated with high hopes and with belief in the future of their countries. Now, fifty years later, I think of the bloodbaths that have marked the history of so many African countries, of political dreams in disarray, and of broken trust. I grieve for dreams lost, and I wonder how many more generations will pass before the hopes I heard enunciated in 1961 will come to pass. Many factors are crucial: educated, able leaders; a sustainable economy; and a viable political structure—then, with it all, a spirit that refuses to give up. Arthur Guiterman, the American poet, wrote somewhat playfully, "Talent made a poor Appearance / Until he married Perseverance."[1] This can be said for the talent of statecraft as well as for that of the poet, the painter, or the playwright.

But what does religion have to do with all of this; or more specifically, what does Christianity have to do with it? Are Paul's words a precious promise that idealists should claim and that believers should invest with eternal meaning?

Obviously I think so, else I wouldn't be including Paul's words in this book. I would remind us, first of all, that Christians have an ultimate stake in all that is good. I carry with me still the philosophy of a pastor in my teenage years who reminded us often that we should "be ready for every good work" (Titus 3:1). My pastor applied this admonition to national and world affairs as well as to delivering soup to a needy neighbor. Paul said, in the verse immediately following our promise, "So then, whenever we have an opportunity, let us work for the good of all, and especially for those of the family of faith" (Galatians 6:10). We dare not give up—not on our political leaders, our business and professional people, our friends and our families, our church and our school. Most of all we must keep believing in our own souls and in God and in God's promises.

Paul's beloved Christians in Galatia disappointed him deeply, but he didn't give up on them. Would he lose with some particular individuals? Almost surely. That's the law of averages, a law that must be recognized but never bowed down to. I concur with the old saying that "you win some and you lose some," but I dare not settle on some losers in advance, and I dare not be content with any of those losses. You and I must keep on hoping, trusting, believing, and working.

Paul was nothing if not a realist, so he reminded us of the danger of growing weary. The legendary football coach Vince Lombardi made famous his conviction, "Fatigue makes cowards of us all."[2] I believe that this is the truth the apostle had in mind when he warned that we might grow "weary." I believe that more battles have been lost by football players in the last quarter, by students in the night before final exams, and by Congress in the hours before recess through weariness than by whatever obstacles the opposition raised. Sometimes weariness needs to be countered by something as ordinary as a good night's rest or even a fifteen-minute nap. But sometimes the weariness is a deep weariness of the soul, an exhaustion that has little to do with our physical re-sources. At such times we need to sit quietly before God, or perhaps take counsel with a trusted, godly friend—or per-haps simply read for a while in a favorite portion of the Bible or a book that lends inspiration. One way or another, the body and soul and mind need to be raised beyond weariness.

And through all of our labors, we need to remember for whom we labor. I'm speaking of both the seen and the un-seen. As a pastor, I kept my eyes on my people, the small and the large, the young and the old, those full of promise and those who sometimes made me despair. As a teacher, I have the same eye for my students. And, of course, be-yond and before my work, I keep my eyes on family and friends; these, after all, are my first trust before God.

But there are also issues in my life that I cannot see but that are altogether real. Causes—like justice and peace—can't be seen, but they are real. And, of course, nothing is as real as God and God's purposes for our world, but God cannot be seen, nor are God's purposes always clear. But I believe—in people and causes and God—and therefore I cannot give up.

So I like Paul's encouraging word, and I have chosen it as one of the promises by which I live my life. Like Paul, I believe in the character of God. That is, I believe that God is on the side of that which is right and therefore that right will eventually win, no matter how strong and how entrenched evil may seem to be.

I have learned, too, that God's purposes and actions are often deceptively simple. I think of a poem-hymn that Percy Dearmer, an English cleric, wrote early in the twentieth century:

Jesus, good above all other,
Gentle child of gentle Mother,
In a stable born our Brother,
Give us grace to persevere.[3]

How strange to look to an infant as a symbol of perseverance! Yet the Christian gospel builds its entire case on such an unlikely formula: not only a child born in undistinguished circumstances but a Savior crucified in shame. The power and purposes of God cannot be measured by our usual human calculations.

Especially in this that God leaves the next to last vote in our hands. I am confident beyond measure that God's purposes will ultimately be done and that if you and I choose to work with God, we will be on the winning side. But it is also clear that God's purposes will not come to pass without our cooperation. The fulfilling of God's will is certain, but the time is left to us.

So I take new hold, each day, on the good promise, and

I know that I must not grow weary in doing what is right, because we will reap at harvest time if we never give up. This promise keeps me in the fight when weariness or time might persuade me to give up.

NOTES

1. Joseph H. Haron, ed., *A Treasury of Jewish Quotations* (South Brunswick, N.J.: Thomas Yoseloff, 1965), 357.

2. Jerry Kramer, *Lombardi Winning Is the Only Thing* (Cleveland: World Publishing, 1970), ix.

3. Elizabeth Knowles, ed., *Oxford Dictionary of Quotations,* 6th ed. (New York: Oxford University Press, 2004), 260.

CHAPTER 11

HOW THINGS WILL
WORK OUT

*We know that in everything God works for good with those
who love him, who are called according to his purpose.*
(Romans 8:28 RSV)

By now most of us have all but forgotten how we felt
in late December 1999. We were standing at the edge of a
new millennium, and although our calendar is a manmade
device, both the most devout and the most secular had a
somewhat eerie, somewhat somber feeling about seeing
what hadn't been seen in a thousand years: all four numbers of the calendar change at once.

But now that a decade of the twenty-first century is behind us we realize that—basically—there was no more difference between 1999 and 2000 than there had been
between 1998 and 1999. And while the media helped us
think of 2000 as a very different kind of change, the future
is interesting whatever the dates—and is always something
of a mystery, full of both foreboding and promise.

As far as we know, we humans are the only part of creation that concerns itself with the future. The rest of
creation simply does what it is supposed to do: it obeys the
rules of the seasons and of nature. But you and I ponder

and wonder, dream and worry. We know that the future is partly under our control and that our acts and decisions do much to shape its pattern. We also realize, however, that many of the most important elements of the future are beyond us: floods and tornadoes and sunshine, war and peace, prosperity and recessions. Some of what happens we can change, but some we simply have to live with. And what do we know about how it will all turn out?

The Bible gives an answer in one of the grandest of all promises, Romans 8:28. To my knowledge no one has ever made a scientific survey about which biblical verses people quote most often, but I dare to venture that this one is somewhere in the top ten. I have placed it at the beginning of this chapter in the Revised Standard Version. I also like the way J.B. Phillips put it half a century ago in his translation: "Moreover we know that to those who love God, who are called according to His Plan, everything that happens fits into a pattern for good." *A pattern for good.* I like that!

This verse is an exciting, encompassing declaration of optimism. When I see together such words as "all things . . . God . . . good," the future looks altogether promising. One can hardly wait to walk into it, in fact.

But we need to pause at the very outset to recognize that this is not an easy Pollyanna philosophy that says simply, "Everything always works out for the best"—which, I think, is the way we often secularize and oversimplify what is in truth a theological statement and a quite profound one at that. Many of our human experiences are not of themselves good nor do they necessarily work out well. Some of our experiences, as far as we can tell, are unremitting tragedy unless there is more to the story than is immediately available. But this Scripture, Romans 8:28, is a substantial, reasonable philosophy of life, and it must be taken in its entirety if it is to be something more than a superficial cheer in the midst of a losing season.

The first, great fact of the promise is this: *God* is at work in the events of our lives and of our world. The verse says,

"We know that in everything *God works...*" How impressive! God is busy just now working in your affairs and mine! Some of us will confess that we have sometimes gotten ourselves into predicaments where we were sure no one less than God could extricate us. Take heart; God is willingly involved in our concerns.

This is one of the most profound and heartening facts I know about our universe as a whole and about our lives in particular. When we declare that God is love, we are making a broad and general statement. When we declare that God is at work in everything that affects us, we're getting specific about it. How much does God love us? We're told that God loves us in the wondrous fact of Calvary and our salvation, but does God's love work also in the details of our daily lives and of the world in which we live? Jesus insisted that it does when he declared that God is interested in the sparrow's fall and in such an insignificant matter as the number of hairs on our head (Matthew 10:29-31).

I am impressed that God is at work in *everything* in our lives. And I am encouraged by this too. Because, you see, a good share of the details of our lives are, of themselves, rather inconsequential. When Dr. Carol Greider received a telephone call telling her that she had won the Nobel Prize in biology for 2009 she was busy folding her laundry. Most of us are doing ordinary things a great deal of the time, even Nobel Prize winners. And I'm encouraged, too, that God is at work in *everything,* because I've come increasingly to realize that sometimes—perhaps more often than we know—the little matters have substantial consequences. Besides, if the little matter is big enough to concern us (as it so often does), it is important enough to gain the attention of our gracious Lord.

The inclusive quality of "everything" encourages me at still another point. The events and happenings of our common days are pretty much a mixed bag. Some are good and blessed in every way from the very outset. Others are indifferent and can be turned to either good or bad. Still others are downright tragic, to the point of disaster. But this wonderful promise, Romans 8:28, encourages us to realize that what counts is not the stuff of which life is made but the One who is involving himself in the stuff. I remember a meal where a teenage boy asked his mother what was in a casserole. She replied, smiling, that if he knew what was in it, he probably wouldn't eat it. That is, a good cook somehow blends together the mix of this and that, and with skillful seasoning and handling, the result is delicious. Here's what I'm saying: God is especially effective in the use of leftovers. God takes matters that of themselves are without promise and somehow makes of them nourishment and hope and strength and wonder. That's what this promise is telling us: God uses everything, including leftovers and discards, as well as good intentions and worthy achievements.

So it is that I rejoice that no combination of circumstances is beyond our Lord. Have you been dealt elements of tragedy? God can shape them into eventual patterns of beauty. Or is all of your life currently adding up to humdrum, so routine that you wouldn't bore even your best friend with it? Wait a bit to see how God can touch and blend these pieces until they gain brilliance far beyond our expectation. And hear this: are you living with the painful knowledge that you've made some stupid mistakes—yes, in truth some wicked ones that ought to be called not mistakes but sins—and now you're paying for them? This remarkable Bible promise insists that God uses all things for divine purposes, making something of even our errors and inconsistencies. Heaven knows that there are times in some of our lives that if God didn't work with poor material there would be nothing at all with which to work.

But—and there is a "but," of course, and you ought neither to be surprised or resentful of it—God expects our cooperation. God willingly works with us, but God expects us to fumble helpfully with the venture. In this, again, the promise is more than mere magic or easy optimism.

So what is it that you and I are supposed to do? Probably a great deal, when one looks at the whole body of Scripture. But this particular verse, this very special promise, mentions two specific things: that we should love God, and that we are called according to God's purpose.

Loving God may seem a strange way for us to cooperate. We think of love as a feeling, but any love worthy of the name means action, contributing cooperation. Because, you see, if we love God we approach life differently. If we come to the daily business of life resenting or doubting God, or if we simply come with cautious indifference, we will deal with the stuff of life in a desultory, indifferent way. So much of our handling of life's issues, minor or major, depends upon the inclination of our hearts. To love God is to rise above cynicism and indifference and easy defeatism and to recognize that since God cares, we ought to care too. And that makes all the difference.

Further, we cooperate with God when we remember that we are among those who are "called according to his purpose." I'm quite sure that one of our greatest human failings is that we don't give enough thought to what God's purposes might be. Indeed, on most days it doesn't occur to us that God is working to any purpose. Some people think that life is "just one fool thing after another," and a great many others think of the purposes of God only when some personal or natural disaster occurs, at which time they quickly conclude that this disaster must be God's will, else why would it happen?

But God has a purpose for our world, and this purpose is *good*. And it is our privilege to work with God in bringing the divine purposes to pass. When we accept the call of God's purpose, we have a compass for life, a compelling and exciting sense of direction. This in itself makes the scattered pieces of life come together meaningfully. If our lives are to make sense, they must have some purpose; no, more than that, they must have the right and highest purpose—a sense of eternal purpose, because we are eternal creatures.

The purpose of God shapes our lives toward good, but it can do so only if we care to cooperate with God's purpose. I remember hearing someone say long ago that when someone greets by asking, "How are you?" that it's popular to answer, "Pretty fair, under the circumstances." This person suggested that such an answer was inappropriate for a Christian because a Christian is never *under* the circumstances. It is our privilege to live *above* the circumstances. We're not to be taken captive by the events and happenings of life. Rather, we bring these matters under the lordship of Jesus Christ.

If God is making all things work together for good, when does the good happen? How long will we have to wait for it? William Barclay observed, from a lifetime of Christian experience, that one doesn't have to be very old before he or she can look back on life and see that some things that once seemed disastrous have worked out for our good and that seeming disappointments prove to be greater blessings. This proves to be true even in instances where we have made bad choices. I often observe that I wish I had been wiser at a number of points in my life and that I had made decisions with better attention to God's will; nevertheless, at this point in my life, I am profoundly grateful that I am where I am. I'm not happy with some of the paths I chose, but I am surprised and blessed by the destination.

I was late coming to know of Julian of Norwich, the great fourteenth-century mystic, which demonstrates again the gaps most of us have at some points in our education. But I will always remember when I first came to know of Julian. Elisabeth Elliott, author and lecturer, had watched through ten agonizing months as her then husband, Addison Leitch, died of a particularly vicious form of cancer. I knew both Elliott and Leitch only by their writings but, moved by the story of his death, I wrote Ms. Elliott of my prayers. I received in reply a letter she was sending to the many persons who had prayed for her during the ordeal. In it she told of the days of his death and of the victory with which he died. She concluded the letter, "I have known the strength of the Everlasting Arms, and with Julian of Norwich, I believe (I am absolutely sure) that 'All shall be well and all shall be well and all manner of thing shall be well.'"

How did Elisabeth Elliott know that "all manner of thing shall be well"? And how, six centuries earlier (in a particularly tragic time) did Julian know it? The evidence was not really there. No one could say, in either case, how far it might be to conditions that could be called *well*. But those who love God and are committed to the call of God's purpose are sure that God will make all things work together for good.

After a long lifetime of seeing God at work in my own life and in the lives of others, and after years of reading church history and biography, I marvel at the way God works with the disparate pieces of life and human conduct to bring good to pass. And the longer I live, the more I marvel, because I have more time to see the chapters of mystery and sorrow unfold into areas of understanding and beauty.

Nevertheless, I must add two qualifying words. The first has to do with the word *good*. My definition of *good* is often poor because my moral vision is poor. I too often measure life by standards of prosperity, immediate satisfaction, and personal gratification. Only with improved vision do I look for—and recognize—more important and strategic good. What seems to me today to be routine or disappointing or even tragic can prove later to be beautiful and of eternal worth.

The second qualifying word is not in the verse, though it surely is implied: *when*. Of course, *when* is always a crucial word in any discussion where faith is involved, because almost everything that is worthwhile takes time. Immediate miracles are very appealing but also very rare. The miracles that demonstrate themselves over time are just as divine even if not as geared to our taste.

The final measure of the purpose of God is not on this earth but in eternity. If I promised you that you will see the good in all of life's happenings during this earthly life, you would know that I was a religious charlatan. Some of the most beautiful contours of our lives will be revealed only in eternity. Happiness on this earth is surely to be desired, but the more significant purpose is in our worthiness for eternity. I'm certain that each of us has some experiences that can never fully prove their worth in this world; only in the light of eternity will their ultimate quality be revealed. Thus, our faith ancestors rightly sang, "We will understand it better by and by."

How will things work out for you and for me? For *good*—for absolute, perfect, and glorious good. Not for a transient good, nor a small and cheap one, but for the good that really, fully, eternally matters. I can't promise that you or I will escape all of life's futilities and sorrows; in truth, I suppose I can promise you just the opposite, that a certain measure of sickness, loss, heartache, and disappointment will come to your life. It's all part of the territory! But I can guarantee that all of these sometimes unattractive elements will work to a purpose. God will make them matter.

Nor will I tell you that God will bring the good to pass unaided. God is counting on our cooperation, yours and mine. The promise of God's good is for those who are called according to God's purpose. We are to be a people of purpose, *God's* purpose, with a sense that we are called to work to God's ends for our time and for ages to come.

So this promise is no easy optimism, no magic. You and I must love God, and we must cherish God's purposes. If we will, we can set God free to work in our lives. God—the eternal God!—will work with us, at the various and sundry places of our lives, and will shape them together with his divine touch until they all come together for good. Some of them in this world, and some in the world to come.

You can count on it. This is how things will work out. For *good*.

CHAPTER 12

WHAT I KNOW FOR SURE

For I know whom I have believed, and am persuaded that he is able to keep that which I have committed unto him, against that day. (2 Timothy 1:12 KJV)

Some of the promises of Scripture have won their place in our hearts and memories because of a particular experience, others because we associate them with a beloved person. I'm about to tell you of a promise that is powerful in its own right but that has engraved itself in my soul because of a hymn and a small public library.

The biblical promise comes from another of Paul's letters, this one written probably during his final imprisonment for his faith. It is, therefore, a kind of spiritual last will and testament. The apostle senses that his life may be taken from him any day. Thus, what he says carries more weight than if he had spoken it at some more ordinary, less ominous time.

The verse became mine (and what makes any biblical promise precious to us is when it becomes uniquely our own) when I was quite young—nineteen years of age, to be specific. I had known the verse for some years; it was in my memory store by no conscious effort, but the natural memory process was helped by the peculiar beauty and rhythm of the King James Version. The King James was the only Bible I knew at that time, long before the proliferation of Bible translations had begun.

I was preaching each evening for a little church in Cherokee, Iowa, in what was advertised as "revival meetings." I'm not sure how much I accomplished in reviving the faith of others during those meetings, but I know how much the two weeks in Cherokee did for my own soul. Sometimes a sermon's best results are those accomplished in the preacher's soul—just as some of the advice we give to others could best apply in our own lives.

I owe special thanks to the public library in Cherokee— a debt so real to me that sixty-seven years later I sent a gift of one hundred dollars to the library that allowed me to check out books in my short stay in their community. I should have sent them more. I think I will do so this year. In one of those books, I read a great preacher's recollection of experiences in his own young manhood in the 1890s, memories of a Bible Conference in New England where the theme hymn was based on 2 Timothy 1:12. Something about that man's story, the library that welcomed me, and the upstairs room near the church where I perspired in Iowa's June heat each day came together to make a verse from the Bible and a familiar hymn a priceless soul heritage. I can't expect you to understand why these quite pedestrian elements came together to make such an impression on my life—but I'm quite certain that you have some such spiritual conglomerate in your soul's heritage too, whether by hymn, by scripture verse, or by simple anecdote. Such is the stuff of which our best memories are sometimes made. They ought, therefore, not be brushed aside but clung to as priceless possessions.

The letter we know as Second Timothy is set in a mood of destiny. As I noted earlier, the letter is seen as Paul's last surviving letter, written from prison and written with the kind of holy foreboding that caused Paul to declare, "I have fought the good fight, I have finished the race, I have kept the faith," and then to declare that he knows a "crown of righteousness" awaits him (2 Timothy 4:7-8). There's a touch of very human loneliness in the lines that follow. He speaks of a situation where "all deserted me," some because of assignments elsewhere and some, like Demas, because they were "in love with this present world." He writes, therefore, as a lonely human being, with all of the emotion a person is likely to feel when he senses the end is near and is therefore doing a soul inventory.

Paul is like Moses on Mount Nebo, looking back on his years of service to God and to God's people and looking toward the shore of eternity. And he tells us his secret, the fire that still burns in his soul. "I am not ashamed: for I know whom I have believed, and am persuaded that he is able to keep that which I have committed unto him against that day." I have before me now the Bible I was reading as a nineteen-year-old, in its second binding but still so fragile that I take it from the shelf only when I want to quote from the King James Version. It is underlined twice, in broken lines that emphasize the significance my soul found in Paul's words.

Men in the work-day world sometimes greet one another with a phrase beyond the usual "Good morning," or "How are you?" One of those extra greetings is, "Whadda' you know for sure?" I don't know if women use the same term; I've not heard one do so. And I have no idea how the phrase was born. It may have come from a time of economic depression or of otherwise devastating testing, or it may have been nothing more than the boyish playfulness that men carry with them on into manhood. But like many phrases that work their way into our common speech, I suspect there's more to it than first meets the ear. We're always looking for something we know for sure. The Apostle Paul had come to know something for sure, and nothing could take it from him.

It's easy to see that life and hell had tried to rob Paul of his certainties. He had been persecuted by his earliest friends and associates—persons who now saw Paul as a theological traitor. He had become a pawn of the political system as his enemies brought him before civil courts for issues that had next to nothing to do with civil matters. Worse by far, many of his fellow Christians had disappointed him, sometimes out of jealousy and sometimes out of disagreement with his teachings and sometimes because of their human inclination to take sides. It's clear that the churches he brought to birth rarely saw him as their favorite preacher even though they acknowledged that they owed their faith to him; nevertheless, they saw other preachers and teachers as more eloquent and winsome. He had no wife, and he makes no reference to his parents. The only family tie to which he refers is a nephew. So what does Paul know, really *know,* in the midst of so many factors that could take life's moorings from him? Just this: he knows *whom* he has believed, and he knows that this one in whom he believes is *able to keep* what Paul has committed to him, and to keep it *against that day*—that is, the day when all judgments will be final.

Paul's declaration is magnificent. He looks circumstances, time and eternity, heaven and hell, in the face and declares that all is well. He knows one thing for sure. Mind you, scores and perhaps hundreds or thousands of other things rest upon this one thing of which he is sure—but this one fact is enough. It forms a base on which all the rest of Paul's believing can be secure.

Daniel Webster Whittle placed Paul's grand affirmation of what he knew alongside that which Whittle happily confessed that he didn't know. He enlisted the help of the musician James McGranahan, a rather popular composer of religious music in the late nineteenth century with whom Whittle often collaborated. McGranahan gave Whittle's words a melody that caught very nicely the spirit of Whittle's convictions.

Whittle was a young bank teller, newly married, when he enlisted in the 72nd Illinois Infantry in the Civil War. He fought in the battle of Vicksburg, where he suffered a serious arm wound. Eventually, he accompanied General Sherman on the march to Georgia, where he was captured and interred in a Confederate prison. After the war he returned to the world of business and while still in his early thirties became treasurer of the Elgin Watch Company in Chicago.

Along the way, Major Whittle came to know the famous evangelist Dwight L. Moody and wrote scores of hymns, several of which are still sung today, well over a century later. I can't judge which hymn is his best. I only know that his personalizing of the apostle's words combined with McGranahan's music has given this hymn special substance and beauty for me. My soul marches to it.

In his hymn Whittle moves systematically through his personal theology, describing in each stanza what he does not know before affirming in the refrain what he knows for sure, using the language of 2 Timothy 1:12 in the King James Version. Thus,

> I know not why God's wondrous grace to me he hath made
> known,
> Nor why, unworthy, Christ in love redeemed me for his own.

And then comes the jubilant refrain: not an answer to the question he has raised but a declaration that makes the question unimportant. And the music itself changes from informative to triumphant and challenging:

> But I know whom I have believed,
> and am persuaded that he is able
> to keep that which I've committed
> unto him against that day.[1]

Having told us that he can't explain why God's wondrous grace should have been extended to him, the lyricist continues in the second stanza to marvel at the manner in which that faith works:

I know not how this saving faith
to me he did impart,
nor how believing in his word
wrought peace within my heart—

After this, again, he launches into the declaration of what he *does* know.

Then Whittle takes a step into still more profound theological territory. Jesus told the scholar Nicodemus that the work of the Spirit of God is like the wind: "The wind blows where it chooses" (John 3:8). Nicodemus answered, in justified bewilderment, "How can these things be?" (John 3:9). Whittle recognized the same mystery:

I know not how the Spirit moves,
convicting us of sin,
revealing Jesus through the word,
creating faith in him—

But he rejoices that he doesn't need to know; he is satisfied to move into the certainties of his refrain.

For a concluding stanza Whittle goes into the complete unknown:

I know not when my Lord may come,
at night or noonday fair,
nor if I walk the vale with him,
or meet him in the air—

But he finds this uncertainty just as inconsequential as all the others, as long as he can affirm with the apostle that he knows in whom he has believed, and knows that his Lord can "keep that which I've committed unto him against that day."

Daniel Webster Whittle had it right, and I dare to think that the apostle would like what Whittle wrote—not necessarily because he would like Whittle's poetic style but because he would feel unity with Whittle's spirit. There are some things we need to know and some things that—while intriguing and perhaps even beneficial—we can live without. Whittle's simple, straightforward lines travel methodically through the issues that occurred to his mind, and in every instance he concluded that however fascinating his questions might be, he could live without the answers; he could live without them, that is, as long as he had a certainty at the core of his soul and of his soul's relationship to God.

Paul's word to Timothy and Daniel Whittle's adapting of the word for his hymn reduced the heart of the Christian faith to a unique issue. That issue is in *Whom*. Christianity has a structure of beliefs, some of them central to all believers, and others peculiar to our individual denominations or faith-groups. These beliefs are important because all beliefs have consequences—and the beliefs that have to do with God and daily life and eternity are the most important of all. But the heart of all doctrine for Christians is in the person of Jesus Christ: his life, his teachings, and his death and resurrection. Thus, in the statement of faith most widely used among Christians, the Apostles' Creed, more than half has to do with Jesus Christ—and the less than half that remains summarizes what Christians believe about God, the Holy Spirit, the church, the forgiveness of sins, the resurrection of the body, and the life to come. It is almost as if the church, in putting together the Creed, was saying what Daniel Whittle said: there is much that we don't know, or that we can leave to some measure of freedom of conscience and interpretation, but one thing is crucial—the Savior, Christ, and our relationship to him.

No wonder, then, that when Blaise Pascal, surely one of the few, true geniuses of human history, recorded the night of his supreme religious experience, he would write, "Certainty. Certainty. Feeling of Joy and Peace. The God of Jesus Christ." For Pascal, the "Certainty" was in Christ. So he would write in his *Pensees,* "Apart from Jesus Christ, we do not know what is our life, nor our death, nor God, nor ourselves."[2]

This is a statement so broad and so inclusive that most of us would raise a skeptical eyebrow if a neighbor or a dinner companion said it; and for that matter, we may struggle with it no matter what Pascal's intellectual or scientific credentials. The skeptic asks, "How can he be so sure?" But of course, Pascal is speaking first of all as a convinced and converted witness. He is speaking in the tradition of the apostle, and is giving his testimony no less than Daniel Whittle—except that Whittle expected that his friend, James McGranahan, would provide a tune for this particular poem-witness just as he had for so many others. Pascal sought no tune. He sewed his statement into the lining of his coat, to be held close to his person in passionate privacy until discovered there after his death. The statement in his *Pensees* that we have quoted is part of the living philosophy of his character and person.

We humans need an anchor for our souls; and because our souls are made of eternal stuff, we need an anchor sufficient to secure such a cargo. You and I live in a culture with any number of temporary anchors—matters that claim a huge share of our time and money and fretful attention but which are often forgotten a few days later. Nevertheless, the voices in our culture insist that we give attention to these transient matters. So we worry ourselves about the demands of fashion (How faded should these jeans be if they are to look properly casual?), the daily state of the economy (The Dow Jones is down today.), and the impression we've just made on a new acquaintance (Did she notice that grammatical slip?). And granted, our lives are made up of all these pieces small and great—most of them small but adding up to our measure.

But somewhere we need to ask ourselves what really matters. On what foundation can we build our lives—especially since our lives have an ultimate, eternal dimension? How much of this can we present to God when we make our crucial stand?

This is the question Paul was answering. At a time

when he had reason to think that his days were numbered, and in a place—imprisonment—where he was compelled to do a continuing inventory of his soul, Paul got to the root of the matter. He realized what most of the time we choose to forget, that a time was coming when he must appear before God. Paul calls it simply "that day"; no other word was needed, because "that day" stands alone among all our days. And some voice asks Paul what he knows as he contemplates that day.

Believe me, Paul knew many things. He knew the Hebrew Scriptures as only a devout first-century Jew (and more particularly, a Pharisee) could know them. He knew a good deal about the Greek and Roman philosophers, so that he could hold his own with the truth-players on Mars Hill. And if you're a down-to-earth person who wonders if Paul knew anything beyond textbooks, I remind you that Paul was a craftsman, a tent-maker; Paul knew how to handle himself in the marketplaces and bazaars of the fast-talking Middle East.

But Paul pushed all of this aside: all of the theoretical, all of the philosophical, all of the survival-practical. Paul knew one thing, *for sure,* and he was betting his life on it: "For I know whom I have believed and I am persuaded that he is able to keep that which I have committed unto him against that day." Paul knew *Whom.* He knew Jesus Christ.

I claim this as one of my precious promises, a promise that holds me. And I like it, especially, when with the help of Whittle and McGranahan, I can sing it.

NOTES

1. Daniel W. Whittle, "I Know Whom I Have Believed," *The United Methodist Hymnal* (Nashville: The United Methodist Publishing House, 1989), 714.

2. Blaise Pascal, *Pensees* (Whitefish, Mont.: Kessinger Publishing, 2004), 129.

Study Guide for
God's Promises That Keep Us
by J. Ellsworth Kalas

John D. Schroeder

CHAPTER 1
NO FEAR OF THE DARK

Snapshot Summary
This chapter shows us how God delivers us from all fears and promises to be our light and salvation in dark times.

Reflection / Discussion Questions
1. Share a fear you had as a child and how it affected your life.

2. Reflect on / discuss the power and promise of Psalm 27:1.

3. What did King David have to fear in his life? How did he cope?

4. List some common enemies that people fear.

5. Why is fear always part of our lives?

6. Reflect on / discuss the many ways in which people cope with fear.

7. What help does God offer us to fight our fears?

8. We all need God's light and salvation. How do we attain it?

9. Reflect on / discuss how and why God's promise conquers fear.

10. What additional thoughts or ideas from this chapter would you like to explore?

Prayer: *Dear God, thank you for delivering us from fear and for being our light and salvation. Help us to have no fear of the darkness, because your power and love sustain us. Amen.*

CHAPTER 2
MY EXPERIENCE WITH TROUBLE

Snapshot Summary
This chapter explores the world of trouble, including how and why it happens, as well as how God promises to sustain us and deliver us during troubling times.

Reflection / Discussion Questions
1. Share a recent experience with trouble in your life.

2. Reflect on / discuss why the book of Psalms has so much to say about trouble.

3. Describe some of the many types of trouble. Which types of trouble are the worst?

4. Why is it easier to get into trouble than to get out of it?

5. Why do some people keep troubles to themselves? Is this good or harmful?

6. What have you learned about trouble over the course of your life so far?

7. Does talking to someone about your troubles help? Explain your thoughts.

8. How can you help someone who is in trouble?

9. How can God help us in times of trouble? What resources does God provide?

10. What additional thoughts or ideas from this chapter would you like to explore?

Prayer: *Dear God, thank you for being there with us in the midst of our troubles. Help us lean on you when trouble strikes and not fear anything, because of your promises and love. Amen.*

CHAPTER 3
A PERFECT DAY, AND WHAT TO DO WITH IT

Snapshot Summary
This chapter uses Psalm 118:24 to explore God's gift to us of brand new days and opportunities. It looks at how we should put them to use and God's promise to us each day.

Reflection / Discussion Questions
1. Describe your own perfect day.
2. Why is Psalm 118:24 a favorite of so many?
3. Give some reasons why this verse could be "one of the loveliest promises in all of scripture."
4. How should we feel about each new day we are given to live?
5. Why is Psalm 118:24 applicable for the whole day, morning and evening?
6. Give some reasons each day is perfect.
7. Why can even a bad day be a good day?
8. Why should we give thanks to God for each new day as we go to sleep?
9. What does God expect from us with the gift of each perfect day?
10. What additional thoughts or ideas from this chapter would you like to explore?

Prayer: *Dear God, thank you for this perfect day and all the perfect days you give us. Help us make the most of every day and grow in love toward you and others. Amen.*

CHAPTER 4
THE WORLD IN GOD'S EMBRACE

Snapshot Summary
This chapter turns to John 3:16 to remind us of God's love for each of us and for all the world.

Reflection / Discussion Questions
1. Name some times in life when we need to remember and recite John 3:16.

2. Reflect on / discuss the meaning and implications of John 3:16. Why is it a favorite promise?

3. According to the author, what is the problem with this verse?

4. What can be learned by breaking this verse apart word by word?

5. When you read John 3:16, how does it make you feel?

6. How is God's love of the world different from our view and love of the world?

7. What lessons can we learn from this verse about the love of God?

8. What does this verse tell us about God and giving?

9. How has God's promise in John 3:16 changed your life?

10. What additional thoughts or ideas from this chapter would you like to explore?

Prayer: *Dear God, thank you for your powerful love of us and the entire world. Help us remember that we are never alone. You sustain us and the world. Everyone and everything is important to you. Amen.*

CHAPTER 5
MERCY FOR OUR POOREST DAYS

Snapshot Summary
This chapter shows us how God promises to be with us when we are downcast, bruised, or broken.

Reflection / Discussion Questions
1. Share a time when you were downcast and how you coped with the situation.

2. Reflect on / discuss how we own, or come to own, biblical promises.

3. How does it feel to be downcast? Why does it often feel like it will never end?

4. Describe some of the many ways in which the human soul can be broken or bruised.

5. Reflect on / discuss how Simon Peter is an example of the truth, promise, and power of Matthew 12:20.

6. Why do the gracious promises of God sometimes turn out to be God's commands?

7. What lessons about mercy can we learn from this verse?

8. Reflect on / discuss how much of Jesus' time and ministry was given to the bruised or broken reed.

9. What can we learn about God and human defeat from this verse?

10. What additional thoughts or ideas from this chapter would you like to explore?

Prayer: *Dear God, thank you for offering us mercy and healing when we are downcast. Help us remember we can always turn to you when we are having a bad day. Amen.*

CHAPTER 6
LIVING IN THE SUNLIGHT

Snapshot Summary
This chapter explores God's promise to free us from condemnation and deliver us into the sunlight of life and love.

Reflection / Discussion Questions
1. List some times in life when people feel condemnation.
2. How does it feel to experience condemnation?
3. Define *self-condemnation,* and give an example of it.
4. Name some of the reasons we often condemn ourselves.
5. Reflect on / discuss the importance of the word *now* in Romans 8:1.
6. What can we learn from the Apostle Paul about condemnation?
7. List some of the truths and promises discussed in this chapter.
8. How should we respond to the message of Romans 8:1?
9. Why is the promise of Romans 8:1 so important for us to remember today?
10. What additional thoughts or ideas from this chapter would you like to explore?

Prayer: *Dear God, thank you for freeing us from condemnation of all kinds so that we can live in the sunlight of your love. Help us remember this promise and celebrate the freedom it provides. Amen.*

CHAPTER 7
LOVE THAT WILL NOT LET ME GO

Snapshot Summary
This chapter reminds us that there are no limits to God's love. God promises to love, sustain, and protect us, so we can always feel secure.

Reflection / Discussion Questions
1. Share a time when you experienced a boundary or limit to human love.
2. What often prevents us from being secure in love?
3. Why can't love always be counted upon?
4. List some of the reasons people long for love.
5. How is the Apostle Paul a realist? What does he say about love?
6. Why can nothing interfere with God's love for us?
7. List some words or phrases that describe God's love.
8. Share a time when you experienced the power of God's love.
9. Name an insight about God's love you learned from reading or discussing this chapter.
10. What additional thoughts or ideas from this chapter would you like to explore?

Prayer: *Dear God, thank you for loving us unconditionally. Help us love others unconditionally. Amen.*

CHAPTER 8
ON BEING A FINISHED PRODUCT

Snapshot Summary
This chapter reveals God's promise and patience to help us grow and mature as we remain works in progress.

Reflection / Discussion Questions
1. Share a time when you longed to be finished with a project or a problem.
2. In what ways do the message and promise in Philippians 1:6 nourish the soul and spirit?
3. Why do people hunger to become a finished product?
4. Reflect on / discuss the story and background of this verse found in Philippians.

5. What does this verse reveal to us about the patience of God?

6. How does God view our potential?

7. How can we help ourselves become more of a finished product?

8. Share what this promise means to you.

9. Name some times in life when it is important to remember this verse and what it promises.

10. What additional thoughts or ideas from this chapter would you like to explore?

Prayer: *Dear God, thank you for all your effort in making us better people. Thank you for your patience as we continue to grow and mature. Help us imitate your love and share it with others. Amen.*

CHAPTER 9
RESOURCE UNLIMITED

Snapshot Summary
This chapter shows us the many resources provided to us by God and how Jesus is the Ultimate Resource for all our needs.

Reflection / Discussion Questions
1. Share a difficult time when you needed God's unlimited resources.

2. Reflect on / discuss both Philippians 4:13 and Philippians 4:19, and what the two verses have in common.

3. Share what these verses mean to you and the power they provide.

4. How does it feel to be in need and to need God's resources? How are God's resources different from those offered by humans?

5. Explain why Jesus Christ is "the ultimate Resource."

6. What do these verses from Philippians tell us about a person's potential?

7. What do we need to do to receive God's unlimited resources?

8. Why are we less likely to look to God for help today than in generations past?

9. Describe some of the resources of God that are available to us.

10. What additional thoughts or ideas from this chapter would you like to explore?

Prayer: *Dear God, thank you for providing for all our needs. Remind us that our potential and your resources have no limits. Help us use all our resources wisely. Amen.*

CHAPTER 10
DON'T GIVE UP!

Snapshot Summary

This chapter reminds us of God's promise to be with us in our struggles, to fight the good fight and never quit.

Reflection / Discussion Questions

1. Share a time when you were tempted to give up.

2. Name some common reasons people give up instead of persevering.

3. Reflect on / discuss why the Apostle Paul is a good example of perseverance.

4. Give some tips for fighting weariness and not giving up.

5. Reflect on / discuss how Jesus demonstrated perseverance in his life and ministry.

6. What is lost when we give up? How are we hurt?

7. Why is it important to always remember for whom we labor?

8. How can God help us persevere?

9. What does it mean that "God leaves the next to last vote in our hands"?

10. What additional thoughts or ideas from this chapter would you like to explore?

Prayer: *Dear God, thank you for encouraging us, cheering us on, and helping us reach our goals and dreams. Help us not give up and also help others in their struggles. Amen.*

CHAPTER 11
HOW THINGS WILL WORK OUT

Snapshot Summary
This chapter uses the promise of Romans 8:28 to remind us that God is in control and that good will always prevail.

Reflection / Discussion Questions
1. Share what the message of Romans 8:28 means to you personally and why it is an important promise.

2. Name some situations in the world today where people are wondering how things will turn out.

3. What part of the future is in our control, and which part is not?

4. Give some examples of human events or experiences that have not worked out well.

5. Explain why the promise of Romans 8:28 is much more than wishful thinking.

6. How do we know that "God is at work in everything in our lives"?

7. Reflect on / discuss the real encouragement that Romans 8:28 offers us.

8. God expects our cooperation to help things work out for good; how can we help?

9. Reflect on / discuss what it means to be "called according to his purpose."

10. What additional thoughts or ideas from this chapter would you like to explore?

Prayer: *Dear God, thank you for reminding us that the world and our lives are in your capable hands, and that things will work out. Help us work for good and lend a helping hand or a listening ear to others when we can. We are your partners. Amen.*

CHAPTER 12
WHAT I KNOW FOR SURE

Snapshot Summary
This chapter explores the Apostle Paul's declaration of the power of God and why we can put our faith, trust, and hope in Jesus.

Reflection / Discussion Questions
1. Share what the message of 2 Timothy 1:12 means to you and why it is a powerful promise.

2. Reflect on / discuss what makes a biblical promise precious to us.

3. What does the author tell us about the letter we know as 2 Timothy?

4. Explain why the author refers to Paul's declaration as "magnificent."

5. Why do humans search for what is sure? Why is certainty so rare?

6. What impresses you about the story of Major Whittle?

7. Explain why we humans need an anchor for our souls.

8. In what times of life is it natural to ponder what really matters?

9. What do you admire most about the Apostle Paul?

10. What additional thoughts or ideas from this chapter would you like to explore?

Prayer: *Dear God, thank you for the certainty you provide in an uncertain world. Help us remember and carry your promises with us in our hearts at all times, and share your promises with others. Amen.*